Heyna's Socialist Wonderland

GROWING UP IN USSR

ANDREJ VOTH

Copyright © 2021 Andrej Voth

All rights reserved. This book or any portion thereof may not be reproduced or used in any manner whatsoever without the express written permission of the publisher except for the use of brief quotations in a book review.

First Printing, 2021

ISBN eBook: 978-1-7779931-1-5

ISBN Print Paperback: 978-1-7779931-0-8

ISBN Print Hardcover: 979-8780100317

www.andrejvoth.com

CONTENTS

Preface	vii
Introduction	ix
1. Blue-Eyed Trust	1
2. My Sweet Family	7
3. Stealing a Gun	13
4. Buying two Hats	19
5. Spiritual Atheist	24
6. The Price of Conviction	31
7. Prophecies of the Future	37
8. Free Medicine	42
9. Cooked Economics	46
10. Essential Rituals	52
11. Concentration Camp Holidays	59
12. For filthy lucre's sake 1	63
13. Abdiel, the Slave	68
14. Death of a Church	73
15. Becoming a Christian	77
16. Baptism at Moonlight	83
17. Driving like a Russian	86
18. Bogomol the Soldier	93
19. Prayer and Promiscuity	99
20. No War, No Love	104
21. A Desert Rose	109
22. Staying Alive	114
23. The Race Card	120
24. Civil Disobedience	124
25. KGB Angels	130
26. Rotting in the West	133
Epilogue	139

Acknowledgments 141
About the Author 143

Dedicated to my sons, Michael and John

PREFACE

These are true stories that take place during my childhood to my early twenties. Most of the names have been changed. I describe events the way I recollect them, which are all totally and subjectively true. This is not a thorough commentary on the sensation known as "the USSR." I did not choose my parents or the country where I grew up. It was handed to me as it was. I know my parents were wonderful, diligent, and very kind. My five siblings and I were very close before we grew up and happily scattered around this beautiful planet.

We grew up together in a country that does not exist anymore. The mighty Union of Soviet Socialist Republics, the USSR. It was a world power that many dreaded. Like any empire, it was ruled by deception, fear, and terror. By its own estimation, it was a wonderful country. A peaceful garden. It disappeared because, in actuality, it began badly and grew immensely evil. As all evil has an expiry date, it too fell and vanished. God, who writes His-Story, turned a page. His patience expired, but God's goodness never actually ceases. Those who search for it will find it in surprising places. A divinely beautiful garden, a place of peace and pleasure, a true Paradise!

PREFACE

Canada, 2021

INTRODUCTION

Exhausted and barely moving my feet, I fell into my bed. The two-week shift in a northern Canadian oilfield fracking camp takes a toll. I drive a heavy water-can truck. Winter is cold here, much like at home, in Siberia.

At my venerable age and after my heart surgery, I should be doing something more easy-going, I thought.

Nonetheless, we could now afford our first home. A 100-year-old dwelling that had been on the market for two years and wanted by no one else. It needed a lot of improvement, and with the help of our son, Michael, it had become our sweet home.

I fell asleep immediately and had a strange dream. My friend Ivan, an experienced hunter, was teaching me the art of the hunt. We saw a dark animal on the horizon. With a single shot, as precise as a sniper, he harvested a giant moose. The antlers were huge. Ivan was happy to be able to go home without having been skunked.

I was holding an AK47 and was spraying gophers with tracer ammo. There were thousands of them and I looked ridiculous. For no apparent reason, I began chasing after a red one. The mammal ran to a hole and jumped in. I peered in, and it was a global-sized, dividing

INTRODUCTION

chasm. Leaning in too far, I lost my balance and fell into the gopher's pocket.

I descended into my boyhood and found myself sitting at my desk in a small Soviet classroom. I was surrounded by my schoolmates and my beloved teacher Tatyana ...

CHAPTER I
BLUE-EYED TRUST

- 1964 -

"We are building a paradise, a wonderland," she said. "You live in the most progressive, fair and peace-loving country of the world – the Union of Soviet Socialist Republics! You are the lucky ones because you will be the generation that will enter into Communism. Our grandparents fought to destroy Capitalists, Bourgeoisie, Fascists, and even now, your parents are sacrificing themselves, all for this dream – the bright future of Communism."

I believed my teacher. I looked up to her. Her name was Tatyana. As a fair-haired, blue-eyed child, I was convinced I was her favourite, and I loved her. She was pretty, but not as much as my mother. She was twenty-something, a sophisticated woman. She had dark hair, dark eyes and wasn't too skinny. A Russian beauty. The woman of my dreams. At a ripe 8 years, this was my second crush. My first crush had been Roza, my neighbour, but at her immature 7 years, she was no match for this goddess.

It was October, the second month of the school year. White shirts and black pants were the uniforms for the boys, while the girls wore black dresses and white aprons.

The school sports hall was filled with students. A small red star with a picture of the sweet, blond-haired Lenin as a child was pinned on each of us. We were elated and felt on top of the world.

Then we sang a "worship" song:

"Lenin lives in my heart. He lived. He lives. Lenin will live forever! Forward to the victory of Communism!" It was a solemn consecration.

The school principal gave a speech, "From today on, you will be called the Children of the Holy October Revolution. Your life goal will be to carry the flag and the hope of Communism to future generations and to all nations on the planet."

Then we sang, "Wide is my Motherland, of her many forests, fields and rivers! I know of no other such country where a human can breathe so freely."

This was a popular song from the Soviet movie "Circus." It told the story of an American woman escaping discrimination in the USA and finding freedom and equality in the USSR.

Running – not walking – home, I proudly displayed the red star on my chest to passers-by. I was impatient to tell my parents and siblings the good news that the "bright future of communism" was upon us. "Brotherhood, equality, peace, freedom! We will not need to lock our doors! Everyone will be honest! No war, no borders, no possessions, only love. We will not need to own anything personally, but everything will be owned by us collectively. We will be happy!"

"The glorious future of the communist paradise is coming to our village soon!" I exclaimed excitedly to my parents as I burst through the door. Papa glanced up, cast a surprised and disapproving look at the red star on my chest, then bowed his head back over his bowl of borscht. I could tell something was bothering him.

"Without God, there will be no paradise, my dear!" my Mama said sarcastically. My heart sank. They are unbelievers, but I know better. I am the new progressive generation! I thought proudly.

THAT EVENING, before bedtime, we sat together, talking and praying. Papa read from the Bible as he usually did. It was illegal to do so. The parable he read was about two builders. One built on sand and the other on stone. When storms and floods came, the house on sand collapsed.

"Build all things in life on a solid foundation, which is the Word of God, and they will last through all times and all trials," said Papa. "Building on sand is what socialists – the godless – do!"

Were the three little pigs socialists? And the big bad wolf, the devil? I wondered.

We all kneeled down and prayed – first Mama, then the children, then Papa. The concluding prayer was regarded as the most important. Then, we went to bed.

My brother Vania and I slept in the kitchen. Papa made a wooden bench that had a big draw. In that draw was a giant bag that Mama filled with straw. We had to even out the straw in the bag and have sweet grass-scented dreams in it.

I loved the stories Papa read to us. I wanted to tell my teacher that she should also read the Bible, but I was afraid she would be mad. And, oh, all the kids would laugh at me and call me a sectarian. I felt sad and fell asleep.

∼

Months flew by, and the school year was ending. Sir Siberian Winter was losing the battles to Mrs. Spring. Spring employed the sun as the most potent weapon. Winter did attack a few times with frost and fog at night, but was losing the war. In obedience to Spring, Sun mercilessly melted the last traces of winter's snow and ice away. The trees started to dress into their best greens, and birds sang their best songs.

Every spring, we had Subotnick, which literally means Saturday Spring Cleaning. Our school organized a Subotnick one Saturday. The school building, the yard and the adjacent park needed cleaning.

It was a sunny day. Walking to school, I stopped in the town center. Young men sat around and smoked and chatted in front of the shops and the bus station. Every passing woman got their attention. They whistled and made suggestive comments.

"Beautiful, do not rush? Come to me, sweetie ..."

"What are you doing tonight? You look gorgeous!"

Some women blushed and said nothing. Some smiled and said:

"Oh, you are so stupid!" or

"Idiot!"

But all of them, without exception, got a fresh spring in their step and a swagger in the hips. Then disappeared in the shops.

One of the guys noticed me standing and gawking at this display of spring flirting. He had a bright and friendly face. He laughed very loudly and shouted:

"Hey, lad, do you like this! Remember, all women are beautiful in the spring, but you need to choose one! That is the biggest tragedy for us men ..." Everybody exploded into laughter.

I shrugged my shoulders and continued to my school.

I don't know what his problem is. Why would one man need a lot of women?

~

AT THIS SUBOTNICK, we all had our chores. Girls would concentrate on the school building. Dust and wipe the ikons (e.i. portraits) of past and present communist leaders. We swept the yard, collected garbage and raked leaves and washed the busts and statues of our revered socialistic gods. They were like huge idols standing there and being absolutely useless. Some heroes needed a fresh coat of paint.

The most impressive was the enormous statue of Lenin in the middle of the park. The birds had used him as their toilet, and he looked awful. So, we washed him and slapped on a new coat of paint.

I had heard Hindus also dress and wash their gods and give them food. We did not provide food but gave everything else to Lenin.

Socialism is a violent religion. So people came day and night to practice it. Under this figure, a lot of things happened. A lot of fights. A lot of drinking. At nights he was used as a toilet. Men and women would come and do things we, as children, were not supposed to talk about.

But Lenin just stood there, dead as a block of cement. Right hand in his pocket, which is a rarity, usually the politicians have their hands in other people's pockets; and with his left hand, he was showing into some undefined future. As if saying: "Someday in the future, everything will be somehow better."

While we were cleaning the cement beneath the feet of Lenin, my cousin Kolja and I didn't notice that we were suddenly surrounded by a gang of children. This was nothing extraordinary – there were many scuffles in our town. Men typically had fistfights; women usually screamed at each other. Children learned from both. On this day, we began with insults and ended up rolling in the mud.

The few gangs in our town were based on nationality. This time, a Chechen mob had attacked us, the Fascists. Our ancestors came to

Russia, now Ukraine, more than 200 years ago from Germany. That was enough to qualify us as Fascists. The reason for contention? Our Russian school principal had mentioned in class that some of us came from the homes of traitors. Outnumbered, we had little chance. Despite flung knives and threats of carrying our intestines in our hands home to our mammy, we fought bravely back. We had bloody noses and scratches, but we still felt victorious as we walked home.

Like the rest of the USSR, our village was a happy, multicultural, harmonious socialist family. Except for the native Kazakhs, our parents had been exiled to this Sovkhoz (a state-owned farm in the Soviet Union). They all were accused of being elements dangerous to the security and stability of our socialist homeland. As the children of Russians, Chechens, Germans, Ukrainians, Moldovans, Chinese, Tatars, Mordvin, and a few other nationalities, we intended to live happily ever after. Sometimes innocent profiling still happened, but only in instances of utter frustration with another custom. Adults generally only fought when drunk, and peace was made over a shared bottle of liquor. Eating and drinking together have a fantastic effect on people, and comradeship is almost always restored.

CHAPTER 2
MY SWEET FAMILY

For the next eight years, school was the primary focus of my life. I managed to not repeat any school years and progressed, albeit tediously, forward. As the third child in my family, my grades were also aggressively average. Most of my siblings were much more intelligent than me and brought home excellent reports, to the praise and joy of our parents.

I had two brothers and three most beautiful sisters in the world. My older brother took all the smarts and my younger brother the looks. I was stuck in the middle with ... well, let's just say I was glad they didn't call the cat or dog by my name! My parents called me Hyena; the cat, Ibrahim; and the dog, Sharick.

Ibrahim, the black cat, led an exemplary socialist life catching treacherous mice and fighting off neighbouring cats' invasions. His ears were round – not because of a noble pedigree, but because the Siberian winters were not kind to the tips of his ears. Ibrahim lived seven long and productive lives. He produced according to his ability, and we provided according to his needs. As he grew old, however, Ibrahim developed ulcers and could not make a fair contribution to our society. He started to cost more than he produced, so he had to be disposed of. Mama asked me to whack the cat. Sometimes I wonder, why me? Was I the natural choice? I did as I was told.

My younger brother Vania, who was a kind boy and an ailurophile, loved Ibrahim. When he couldn't find his favourite pet, he was told the cat had run away. Until spring, all was quiet, but you cannot hide your sins forever. The snow melted. On one of Vania's long strolls through the village backyards and alleys, he discovered the gruesome, preserved sight of his beloved Ibrahim's frozen body. With clenched fists and fury in his teary eyes, the small boy came storming into the kitchen. He attacked me, the executioner, and screamed at the top of his lungs, "Murderer! Killer! Assassin!" I still wonder – why did he assume that it was me? Perhaps that's why we live on two different continents today.

Sharick, the canine, who was also black and always smiling, guarded our house and goods from corruption, thieves and drunkards. Vania loved this canine as much as he loved all of God's other creatures. So much so that when our mother could not find Vania, she quickly learned she would find him in Sharick's kennel, curled up and sleeping with the dog.

My memories of Sharick are also associated with my older brother, the professor. I would play with Sharick outside and observe Yasha sitting inside by the window. He was always experimenting with physics formulas or chemistry tests, or building a weapon. His obsession was the North American indigenous tribes. He had read everything and anything available in the limited Soviet literature and compiled many handwritten notes. Editions on lives, traditions and hunting practices filled several handwritten volumes. He was quite often severely focused on his work and not very playful. This provided an excellent setting in which to annoy him, something I thoroughly enjoyed!

One day, after I had once again interrupted his scientific experiments, the vexed academic chased after me. Trying to escape, I ran past the massive pile of coal that we used to heat our house in the winter. I did not make it far. A mighty kick catapulted me onto the top of the black mountain. I landed face down, my tears and pain mixed with the black coal dust. I had learned an important life lesson – never make fun of science because scientists always win.

Winter came, and I joined Yasha as an assistant for a hunt he had planned. We manufactured a spear. An old, sharpened, triangular file from our father's toolbox served us perfectly. We hid in the field behind our cattle barn and waited for the stray dogs who were always hungry and looking for food. When one of the poor creatures strolled into our snow-covered potato field, my "Indian" brother propelled the spear. The dog got a mighty scratch, yelped, and ran away. Yasha gave a loud war howl and glared in my direction. I knew it was somehow my fault that he would have nothing to skin that night.

Once a week in our town, we had a movie night. They were mainly World War II movies. However, Christian children did not go to the cinemas. Films were seen as a socialist propaganda tool of the government. Christians guarded their children against indoctrination as much as possible. Still, despite being the leaders of the conservative Baptist Church, my parents were soft on us and occasionally gave in to our pleading. So, once or twice a year, I would go to a movie night in our local town's clubhouse. The story was almost always the same: a few handsome Russians killing a bunch of Germans who were either stupid, ugly, skinny soldiers or fat, sweaty, bespectacled officers. Many years later, after we were expelled from the glorious USSR to the Rotten West, the first movie that I saw in the USA was "The Inglorious Bastards" (1978). I thought, I already saw this movie in the USSR! They have stolen the script from the Russians. These are the same good-looking Americans and the same stupid-looking Germans. What a small world!

Sunday came, and as on every Sunday, we had church. "Sunday" in Russian is "The Day of Resurrection of Jesus Christ," or "Voskresenie," so the atheists, who came to disrupt and persecute the believers, had to make plans to raid the Christians on The Day of the Resurrection. Religious gatherings were against the law, but meetings were held in the homes of believers on a rotational basis. At our house, we carried most of the furniture outside in the summer. Next, wooden benches were organized in rows. Meetings were generally in the mornings. Only when the militia raids intensified did we alternate days, places and times. Sometimes we met at 4am.

The three sermons delivered that Sunday were about the inability of humans to find the way back to God's paradise by their own principles of logic. God provided the way, the truth and the life through Jesus Christ.

Adam and Eve, our ancient parents, decided to exclude God from their lives. To become, so to speak, godless. The charming Red Socialist Serpent had promised them freedom from God, equality with God, and the ability to decide for themselves what was good or bad. Adam and Eve believed the sales pitch and eventually lost everything they had and more. As most people never learn from history, we are doomed to repeat the fatal mistakes of the past. The USSR was another repetition of the same foolish decisions.

We were told that the resolution to travel on the highway to Hell was a personal choice, and to climb the stairs to Heaven was hard, but also a personal choice. You decided which way you progressed.

Being honest with God was the starting point. Switch sides. Pray God to be the Lord of your life. Fire the Serpent as your advisor. Ask God to forgive you for the sin of working to make it on your own.

Followers would cry, repent and pray. The new converts were congratulated and assured that their lives would be more dangerous from here on. They were now citizens of the heavenly country, and the earthly empires would not accept them. To be discriminated against and ostracized was a badge of honour for a true believer.

After several hours of church, we ate a lavish meal together. Older adults strolled home for a nap. Kids and young adults hung around singing, telling stories and discussing intriguing topics.

Feelings of happiness, acceptance and belonging filled my heart. My knuckles hurt, my eye was swollen, and my nose still felt tender from the week's battles, but I felt safe, loved, understood, and at home. These people were true friends, I thought. They called me a sinner but loved me as a saint.

Still, I thought it was strange. Whenever atheists talked about socialism and the future utopia of Communism, I felt encouragement, empathy and patriotism. However, I loathed the hatred they spewed and the fights they constantly caused.

Here, in church, I felt condemned by "the holy gaze of God." I was a wretched sinner, but I bathed in love and genuine care. Undeserved grace felt much better than a merited victory. Before going to bed that night, I read:

Faithful are the wounds of a friend who corrects out of love and concern, But the kisses of an enemy are deceitful because they serve his hidden agenda. Proverbs 27:6 (In English from the Amplified Bible)

CHAPTER 3
STEALING A GUN

- 1965 -

"You have to call your Papa and come quickly!" Boris was shouting and motioning with his hands. "My father is drunk and insists that you come!"

Boris lived with his brother Tolik and sister Aigul just across the street. Their father, Mustapha, was an imam, a Muslim worship leader. They were good neighbours, and Boris was my best friend. I found my Papa and said, "Papa, Mustapha said he wants to see you."

He dropped a spanner on the ground, wiped his greasy hand on a rag, and stretched his back. He was always working on somebody's motorbike or car in his spare time. As the best mechanic in our community, he could fix anything. The soviet technology needed constant loving care.

Papa slowly started walking across the street towards our Muslim neighbours. In this culture, to refuse an invitation could be easily interpreted as rudeness or disrespect. A few of us children trotted behind him like ducklings. Mustapha's property was about the same size as ours. The difference lay in our veggie gardens, apple trees and potato fields. Their yard had a solid fence and many animals: plenty of sheep, several cows and four horses.

It was a Muslim feast, and the yard in front of their house was full of people. Relatives and friends came to celebrate and stayed for several days. Sitting on low stools or on the ground, some drank tea, smoked, and simply talked. Boris told me later that his parents always complained about how expensive it was to feed and house all these visitors. But the law of hospitality is a must, not a choice.

"My esteemed neighbour, Ivanovich, I am honoured you came to see me!" Mustapha shouted, approaching and greeting Papa. He had had a few shots of vodka and was visibly annoyed.

"I have called you because I want to give you a gift of friendship," he was still holding on to Papa's hand. "We are both God-fearing and worship the Almighty. To honour you, I am giving you my best stallion! Please accept my humble gift!"

"Boris, go get the Farah (meaning Joy) and bring him quickly," he commanded his oldest boy. Farah was the best horse he had.

"Mustapha, my good neighbour, I appreciate your generosity, but what would I do with such a beautiful stallion as Farah? Keep him. Do not part with him and keep him for your sons," Papa politely refused.

"Oh well, oh well, if you insist. But what about a cow? You have a lot of mouths to feed. Certainly, you will have good use of it and accept a cow!" he changed his offer.

"No, I do not need a cow – I already have two of my own. Thank you. It's very kind of you."

"I cannot let you go without a gift, my friend," insisted Mustapha, "I have to give you at least a sheep. Please accept my small gift to you."

Boris and I were standing and watching our fathers engage in a game of polite cultural exchange. Everyone else was also watching the two men intently. One, a Christian preacher, and the other, a Muslim teacher. Both sincerely respected and genuinely liked each other. In the face of the atheistic socialist dictatorship, believers in God of various religions had a truly heart-felt affinity for each other. A believer in God had a spiritual dimension to his persona. A God denier was seen as stuck in his primitive animalistic state.

My Papa continued to refuse to accept the gifts and was bringing the conversation to a close. "My friend, I am not in need. The good Lord has provided, but I know that if my family is in a dire situation, you will not refuse to help. As I will be prepared to help you at any time. However, today, I am not in need! Thank you for your generosity!" and he started to walk back to our house.

Mustapha turned to his relatives and started to berate and shame them in a loud and angry voice. "Look at that, my relatives! This holy man shows respect and does not want to take anything that IS MINE! But you, scoundrels, just sit here and are prepared to eat me poor. If I offered you what I have submitted to my neighbour, you would take everything without hesitation and leave me destitute on the street. Shame on you! Shame! You should all pack up and go home …" Mustapha carried on and on for a while, embarrassing and scolding his relatives.

Boris motioned for me to follow him. We went into the house, where it was darker and more relaxed. I liked their home because it was so different from ours. They had almost no furniture, and everything was covered in beautiful Persian rugs. Perfectly soft to walk on and to sit to drink strong milky tea or eat sweets.

Today, several women were sitting on the floor and making kurts. A kurt is a snack made of salty cheese. The women lifted their skirts, exposed their thighs and, grabbing a handful of cheese from a bowl, rolled it into small balls on their thighs and placed them on a tray. After, the kurts dried in the sun. Boris grabbed a few and ran out the door as his mother slapped him on the back of his head. I followed. He gave me a few kurts to snack on.

We walked into a big summer room adjacent to the house, and Boris pointed to a chest. The chest was well used and large. Opening it, he searched inside with his hand and pulled out a single barrel shotgun.

"What?!" I exclaimed, "What do you use it for?" Most people in the Soviet Union did not have guns. The government did not like citizens to be armed.

"Father goes hunting ducks sometimes," he said dryly. He put the barrel back among the rags and junk. Nature magazines featured pictures of hunters with single and double-barrel shotguns. To own a gun looked romantic and admirable. I dreamed that one day I would own one.

We walked out into the hot summer sun. The loud arguing and discussions continued in the yard. They talked in the Kazakh language, and I understood only a few words. I tasted the kurt snack, and it was bitter and salty. When everyone was looking in another direction, I threw the brown kurts into the bushes. I didn't like the taste and was worried about getting thigh hair between my teeth.

I WALKED out onto our street: Maxim Gorky. The cross street was still wholly flooded after the last blast of rain, so I turned and walked towards the centre. It was a scorching afternoon. The bakery and a cake shop where Papa worked were two blocks away. You could see the hot air rising from the heated street, and not a soul was in sight. Locals said that only stray dogs, white fools and the mentally sick walked outside at this time of the day. I saw a figure turning into our street and walking toward me. I thought I was not alone; there was another insane one.

It was my cousin, Igor. Upon reaching me, he gestured to sit down under the shade of a tree.

"What's up?" he asked, looking away. He was bored, like me. It was a summer school break, and a lot of us were looking for adventure.

"My neighbour has a shotgun," I informed him. We sat quietly for a moment.

"We should steal it," Igor said, still looking somewhere else.

"Why?"

"Because!"

"To do what?"

"We could go hunting. It could be good for self-defence."

He was a year older than me, and I reckoned he was more intelligent. With my 9 years of life wisdom, I was unsure what to hunt for and what to defend against with a single-barrel shotgun, but I liked the idea of having a gun. So, we devised the perfect plan to snatch the object of our desire.

The next day one of us distracted the family, and the other walked the gun out. I was surprised by how easy stealing was. Our goal had been achieved. We hid the gun in our cattle barn and began brainstorming our next steps. The unanimous decision was that we needed ammo.

Weeks passed. We could not source the 12-gauge ammunition. We didn't know where to buy it or whom to ask. Boris asked if I knew where the gun was. I lied and said that I didn't. After a few weeks, our excitement at having a shotgun faded. The only thing left was increasing feelings of guilt. Why did we do this? Really? No one really needs a gun. Stealing? Lying? Taking what is not ours? Don't I know better? The nagging thoughts bothered me.

Laying at night with open eyes and feeling ashamed of being a thief will take the joy out of even a boy like me. Talking to my parents was a bad idea, I thought. It would only make them miserable. It also had the potential to ruin our good relationship with our Muslim neighbours. It would be selfish to ease my conscience with a confession and burden others with something I had done wrong. As a Protestant denomination, we practiced private and public confessions of sin. Still, my Papa was the one to whom people came to confess. There was no alternative, I thought, and so I was silent.

Another few weeks passed, and the fun with the gun was gone completely. Our family had a small garden of Siberian crabapple trees. Being a bit of a loner, I sometimes liked to wander around and daydream in there.

One day when I was by myself, sitting under a tree, I felt an eerie sense of something beside me – but did not see anyone. A ghost? An angel? Not terrifying, but awe-inspiring. I had heard of spirits and of The Spirit. This powerful presence was pure and exuded calm, but at the same time, it was judging me.

"What do you want from me?" I whispered. I felt the hair on my hand lifting. "I am a sinner. I am a thief and a liar," I started involuntary confessions.

"Return what is not yours," I heard. "Make right what is wrong."

The following day I walked across town to Igor's house. I sat on the house steps and waited until he came out.

"We need to give the gun back," I said.

"I don't care," said Igor. He also had no idea what to do with it.

We carried out the reverse trick and placed the shotgun in its owner's old chest that same day. No one knew except us. My conscience had become my enemy. Like an inner preacher, it would now accuse me of being sinful. It was a maturity milestone. From then on, I knew I was not an innocent child; I could be bad.

CHAPTER 4
BUYING TWO HATS

Papa was very respected in our town. He was a well-known Christian minister, an electrician and, as I mentioned, a good mechanic. My parents lived by the bible principle of doing good to as many people as possible. One day a grateful person stopped by with a truck full of grain. This was also called "oiling the connections."

Papa looked displeased and asked, "What is this?"

"It is for you, my friend. I know you have chickens, geese and cows. It is for the winter. I know you need the feed. It is simply a 'thank you from me."

Now, it was evident that he had not grown it himself. It was harvest time, and he was trucking grain from combines to the silos. Officially it belonged to the Sovkhoz, but in "reality," it belonged to all of us, the proletariat. It was, but it also was not stealing. It depends on your philosophical point of view.

"You know I am a Christian, and I will not accept it. Thank you, but no."

"Oh, do not insult me!" he played the victim. "You know I do not steal. It is only for you, my friend."

I leaned on the fence, observing the exchange between Papa and the young, muscular driver. I felt sorry for the truckie. Papa was a very blunt and straightforward man. Facts and truth always triumphed over sentiment.

"Well then, don't accept it for free. Give me three rubbles, and we are quits," the man begged. Three rubbles was the price of a bottle of vodka.

"No, thank you, you can go now," Papa repeated. The generous fellow made a sad face and slowly peeled off to look for someone else to bless.

"Papa, he only wanted to be nice to us," I said.

Papa: "No, stealing is stealing my son! We don't do that!"

"But Uncle Ury is a Christian, and he brought a load home!" I was pushing my luck.

Papa stared at me and replied," What others do is none of your business. We do not do it! You will never do it! Do not compare yourself to others! Walk before God, not people!"

The national sport was drinking booze, telling sarcastic jokes about the government and cheating the system. "No, it's not stealing! In socialism, everything belongs to everyone, right?" It was said that the Communist Party First Secretary Brezhnev was once asked what to do about the problem of looting that had grown to enormous, uncontrollable proportions. Everyone was stealing what they could.

"When they steal, where do they take it?" Leonid Ilyitch Brezhnev asked.

"They take it home, and they sell some on the black market," was the response.

"They don't take it abroad to other countries, do they?" he tried to qualify.

"No!"

"Well. Let our patriots steal. It still stays in the country!"

The synonym words for stealing were, "it just followed me home" or "it transferred." Everyone was equally poor, so creative thinking was a necessary survival skill. This survival instinct is very deeply ingrained in an ex-soviet mentality. If you achieved something the conventional way, it was okay. Still, if you could undertake something illegal in the process and not get caught, this was viewed as absolute mastery.

∼

Yasha came into the kitchen and said to Mama, "There are a few leather hats on sale in the shop."

"Heyna, dash and buy two. One for Yasha and one for yourself," said Mama.

I started to make fun of Yasha and the urgency he had to buy before they sold out. Mama looked very cross with me, but I noticed she enjoyed the fun. Yasha got annoyed and shoved me towards the door. I ran to the town centre and into the government-run shop (private shops did not exist, and anyone who started his own selling enterprise was labelled a "speculant" and subject to profiteering criminal charges). All shops were divided into two sections by a wooden bar. On one side were the goods and the clerks, and on the other, the customers. Canned fish, vodka, candies, salt, and sugar were almost always available. Black and gray bread could be bought in the mornings, and luxuries only on certain Soviet holidays. If there was a lineup, you did not ask why, but joined it to reserve a spot. Only then would you ask,

"What's on sale?" or, in the local jargon, "What did they throw out?"

Then you would be told that sausages, meat, fresh fish, apples or some other exotic good had been trucked in.

Sometimes you knew that they had something, but it was not on display. You would ask the salesgirl very politely,

"Devushka (girl), do you have leather hats?"

"No! Are you blind? Don't you have eyes! Stupid!"

"Oh, sorry, of course, of course, but Yasha said you do!" I insisted. I knew the game with this girl.

She pretended to ignore me and walked into the backroom/warehouse. Came back and asked: "How many?"

"Two!"

"Here," she threw them on the counter. I dropped the money and ran out.

On the street, a male voice was loudly moaning and complaining.

"Who will rescue me from this crazy woman! Oh, oh, that hurts! Stop it, you mad woman!"

Artem was a two-meter-tall middle-aged man slowly strolling away from his wife Soya, who was short and reached only to his waist. She was following him with a long stick. Artem covered his head with his hands, and every time a blow landed on his head or back, he groaned, "Oy, oy, oy ... please save me from this deranged woman!"

I stopped to watch the comedy alongside others. It was funny and sad at the same time. They both were well known as the most gifted artists and craftspeople in town. They would create beautiful murals and mosaics in shops, offices, and houses for our society's upper class (sorry, the "more equals"). Consequently, they were paid big money, which they dutifully spent on booze. The creative productions were then halted. When the cash and alcohol dried up, Madam Muse would return, and the creative process would resume.

"What did you source today?" asked Uncle Pasha.

"Leather hats," I replied.

"Oh, good! But did you know, in Moscow, in the basement of the Kremlin, they have a huge supermarket where the elite can help themselves to anything under the sun?" He liked to show off his knowledge and give anyone who listened to him a piece of his new information.

"What can they buy that we don't have here?" I wondered.

"Oh, you know – absolutely nothing," he said as he rolled his eyes. "Only everything that they have in the spoiled, capitalist countries and more. Exotic fruits, delicacies, meats, caviar and sweet gourmet foods! French wines and whisky from Scotland!"

"Uncle Pasha, I really don't know what you're talking about," I said. The many foreign words had made me wonder.

"Oh, and did you know that this market was founded by our Fuehrer Vladimir Iljitch Lenin himself? And that he secured the prices in the 1920s, and our communists are so faithful to his decrees that they keep those low prices today? What you buy here for one rubble they can buy for 1 kopeck!"

"I have to go. Mama will be worried", I said and ran home.

I asked Mama if she knew of the secret market in the Kremlin's basement. She just said that Moscow was not Russia. It was a world to itself, and the communist elite lived better than the Tsar, and his family ever had. "I believe that they pretended to arrange to take a picture and sat the Tsar's family in a row against a wall. Then they pulled out their revolvers and shot the kids and the parents," she said.

I didn't want to listen to the conspiracy theories and went outside to stroll barefoot on our dusty, but to my mind, very progressive village streets.

CHAPTER 5
SPIRITUAL ATHEIST

- 1966 -

Papa came home and said," There will be persecution coming. We had a difficult meeting today with an Über-Presbyter Orlov. "

The Über-Presbyter, Lev Orlov, explained the new rules to our church's board of elders. A small, bald, chubby man in a gray coat spoke in a high-pitched voice. He felt powerful, and he enjoyed it. Despite this, he sat on the edge of his chair and looked a bit nervous – the sort of man who would have no power in real life or on the streets. Insecure and fidgety, he would only ever find a career in religion or politics, where his performance could not be objectively measured. He had come from the regional capital to advise the leaders of our church on how to become an officially recognized church in the socialist society.

"There are certain things you cannot talk or preach about anymore. So, you will drop from your sermons the Second Coming of Christ, for example," said Lev Orlov. "You know that does not bode well with the communist progressive plans of building a utopian paradise here on earth," he smiled. "You still can believe it in your heart, but do not talk about these doctrines in church or in public! Now, here is a complete list of Christian dogmas that do not align with the politically correct views."

"There are also specific rituals that many Christians undertake, which are now outlawed. You should never evangelize or promote Christianity," he smiled again. "You also cannot baptize young people, you cannot teach children the Bible, you will have to reduce your choir and communal singing ..." He went on and on.

He revelled in the sound of his own voice, listing with glee all the rules and regulations of the godless government designed to suppress God-worshiping people. He was a representative of the spiritual atheists, whose job it was to regulate the religion of the "primitive, uneducated and superstitious" peasants.

The monotoned, self-indulgent talk of this manikin was periodically interspersed with a smile and dull-witted look. The temperature in the room slowly was rising to boiling point. It did not take long for papa, who was in general, not a very patient man, to lose his cool. Other elders joined in and told the guy in no uncertain terms to get out and get back to where he came from.

"Never come back," they said.

"The demands you outline are treacherous, non-biblical, anti-Christian! You call yourself a minister of the gospel? You are a Judas yourself!"

"With these conditions, we will never register or become official." From that moment, our church obtained a so-called "underground" status.

Well, it was a courageous but not politically smart move. The thin skin of this "Über-Presbyter" had been pierced. He was in bed with the secret services who would move into action on his behalf. Understandably, he felt insulted and humiliated by these backward religious fanatics. He hurried to his Volga (the most luxurious soviet car), and his chauffeur whisked him and his inferiority complexes away to the safety of his atheist friends.

What had happened here was an instance of two different interpretations of the Holy Scriptures: one viewed the Bible as a valuable but adjustable tool to respect God and serve the government. The other viewed the Bible as the ultimate, unchanging authority of life to recognize the government and serve God.

Months before this meeting, our town government official had approached the leaders of the growing church in our small town. He explained that a civic organization, in this case, the church, needed to be officially registered with the authorities.

The board of elders agreed to do so. They asked for the necessary documents and began to prepare the application. Still, nothing is simple in a socialist bureaucracy. To mix it up and make things complicated, there has to be an expert, a self-proclaimed scientific specialist. And this was the visit of the Über-Presbyter from the oblast.

This event kick-started an upset of persecution, discrimination, betrayal, fines, arrests and imprisonments. A spiritual atheist who claims to be tolerant, accepting and enlightened will never stoop down to offer these graces to a person that does not submit. Mercy is shown only to slaves. Independence was labelled as rebellion and needed to be crushed.

First, they started to ridicule and interrogate children in school. Parents protested, but children of believers were effectively becoming outcasts. Mobbed and bullied by teachers and other students, we would often come home in tears. We started receiving bad notes and reports, despite overall good performances.

~

"STAND up when I am talking to you, schoolboy!" the teacher screamed at me. I stood up and looked down. I dreaded what I knew was coming. Tatyana, my lovely teacher, my crush, was fast morphing from goddess to witch.

What happened to her? I wondered. Even her face is transforming from a beauty to a beast.

"What do we hear?! Is your daddy a sectarian? He believes in God and teaches others to follow this scam of lies. He probably has a secret ... an enemy of our glorious state, and a pervert!" The sarcasm and untruth hurt. She went on and on. Some students joined in and laughed at me and at what she said. Others, from Muslim and Christian families, were quiet and looked scared.

The next day our classmate, Fedya, a big guy from a Yakut nation, had not done his homework. That was not unusual for him. Mathematics was taught by our quick-witted Chinese teacher, Nikolay. We liked him, he had a lot of fun and gave good illustrations during his lessons.

"Why didn't you do your homework? Do you want to be as stupid as your parents are?" Nikolay asked mockingly.

"My parents aren't stupid," said Fedya. He wiggled free from his narrow chair-table combination and stood up, like a mountain when compared to the teacher. You could tell he was not afraid. He looked furious.

"Well, what does your dad do? Drive a tractor on the farm?! You do not need much brains to do that! But you, young man, need to study to be a cosmonaut – to fly into the cosmos, for the glory of the USSR!" the teacher said, fulfilling his role as an agent of indoctrination.

Fedya was losing his cool, and he stepped forward, threatening the teacher. We all shouted," Fedya, Fedya, don't do something stupid!!"

The bell rang, and the class was over. Nikolay said to Fedya, "Please come into the teacher's dressing room right now." He was vividly angry and clearly felt disrespected.

We all assembled outside the door to see what would happen now. Fedya was self-assured and slowly opened the door and walked into the teacher's dressing room. Immediately, we heard a loud thump, and Nikolay walked out. Paying no attention to the crowd, he went upstairs to the principal's office. We rushed to open the door and saw Fedya lying on the floor, knocked out.

It was a lesson for all of us - respect your teachers!

A day after that, I was told to go to the principal's office. Oh no, I thought, what now? Upstairs, I saw a boy and a girl from our church and quickly understood that it was about our beliefs. We were called in, and we were told that our parents were also stupid. At least they are not hitting us as they did Friday, I thought. Words are unpleasant, but I will try to forget them. I tuned out the litany of the principal. Like a radio, it became background noise, and I fled into my world of fantasy. It had to be done discreetly so that nobody would notice. It was very effective and helped keep me steady. A valuable skill that I had learned.

I was growing up, and I had started to notice the character traits of my father (and maybe my ancestors) in myself. I liked that, and it felt like a compliment to be like them. Impatience, a short fuse and intolerance for someone full of himself, I thought, were good attributes. Evil is inconsiderate and is a constant violent part of a proper socialist society. Evil people will always exist. So, the best life skill was to stay under the radar, lurk in the shadows, and remain unnoticed. Evil is an aggressive predator, and it eventually seeks you out and challenges you. To stop and confront it, good people have to become skilled in violence themselves.

Yasha said that at work, Christians were called to visit the office of the newly arrived inquisitor. A wide range of questions were asked:

Who are the leaders of the church?

Who teaches the children?

Who conducts the church choir, who reads The Bible and prays publicly in the church?

What are the names of the preachers?

In whose houses, and how often do you come together to practice your sectarian rituals?

Do you have orgies?

Do you sacrifice children?

Do you drink the blood of infants?

Do you have connections to western countries?

Who is a spy for western aggressors?

Do you collect tithes?

Where do you get your religious literature?

Everything was recorded to be used in court. Some began to lose their jobs, but in the USSR, not having a job meant you were a parasite and a criminal and could be persecuted as such. Some were financially fined. Some said nothing. Some cried. Some doubted.

A good portion of the church members sold their houses and what else they could and left town. Some collaborated and treacherously slandered the leaders and active members of the church.

We cannot choose what happens to us in life, but we can choose how we react to events. Choices were made, and lines were drawn.

We gathered at my uncle's house and were listening to a sermon. Suddenly, bricks came flying through the windows and drunks shouted obscenities on the street. "Hey, bogamoly (God-Worshipers)!" they screamed. "Come out. We wanna talk to you!" Some of our young men wanted to go out to calm things down, but others stopped them to prevent a brawl. Tensions grew. The indoctrination of locals began to take effect, and violence and hatred increased. The division of classes and society, always a valuable tool in socialism, was effectively implemented again with all the predictable results. Religious people were classified as enemies, and those who sided with atheism were classified as heroes with common sense.

In several services there was a sudden invasion of officials. The school principal would come in and make a list of all children in the service. Managers would make a list of workers who attended the services. KGB agents noted down preachers, leaders and choir conductors.

Fines were increased. Peer pressure at work intensified. Schools did their best to abuse and demoralize children.

CHAPTER 6

THE PRICE OF CONVICTION

It was an early summer morning in June 1966, about 7 am. The cows were already on the grazing fields, and the village shepherd was taking care of them. There was a loud bang on the front door. The house was surrounded by militia. Regional KGB and local officials came in. "We have a search warrant," they announced loudly.

Mama was standing in the middle of the room. Papa got up and sat on a chair, as ordered. One by one, we kids started to wake up. Peering through our sleepy eyes, we wondered what kind of early visitors they were. Everyone looked puzzled and scared. My two younger sisters started to cry.

"Tell the kids to shut up," a young officer commanded. He looked nervous. He was a young man in uniform just doing his duty. I hoped he knew that we were no criminals. Still, under the spell of propaganda, he felt he was fulfilling a holy task.

We all were not allowed to leave the house or touch anything. Then the detestable men began to search through the house. They were not locals. There was still enough human decency in our community that most would not have the ugliness within to treat their neighbours in such a disrespectful manner. When enlisting young men into military or special forces services, the Soviets made sure to move them thousands of kilometres across the country: from Siberia to Ukraine, Ukraine to Kyrgyzstan, Kyrgyzstan to Moscow, and so on. They knew that a son would not use force or weapons against his relatives and friends, but it wouldn't be a problem in a different region.

Drawers were opened, valuables were thrown from shelves, kitchen cupboards, and the house turned upside down. Anything that could be used in a religious ceremony was placed on the table in front of the officers. Bibles, handwritten songbooks, and biographies of holy people were all confiscated. Most books had been printed in the underground secret printing presses. Any piece of paper that had the word God, Christ or anything religious on it was confiscated. Everything was listed and recorded.

Our house had three rooms. One was the kitchen-dining-laundry, another the living-room and bedroom for the boys, and the last, our parents' and sisters' bedroom. From under my parents' bed, they pulled out an electrical voltage meter. The electricity supply was irregular, and there were surges. Papa worked as an electrical mechanic and kept some tools at home. To keep them at work was unsafe due to thieves.

The voltammeter was placed before the esteemed officer. He looked triumphantly at Papa and with great satisfaction pronounced,

"You are an American spy! Now we have your powerful radio with which you communicate with your western bosses. You are an evil traitor to the Soviet Union!"

No one dared to disagree with this ridiculous, distorted, and untrue statement. Twisting facts was a finely honed skill of the socialist, and everyone present knew this was just a tool and not a radio. Still, all nodded at this description of a "despicable act of treachery." They were happy that they had found some much-needed evidence and could finish their awkward and embarrassing house-search exercise.

This was then framed as a very clever, covert operation. No one would ever suspect that a vicious "spy" would open up shop in a remote small village on the Kazakh/Siberian border. Thousands of kilometres away from any national borders. There were no military or industrial complexes. No cultural treasures. No government departments. No educational or media institutions. Only wheat, herds of cattle, sheep and goats, nomads on horses and endless dirt roads. This man, who had three years of schooling, six years of GULAG experience, worked in electromechanics, read the Bible and prayed with friends on the weekends, was a "sleeper spy" and an absolute danger to the stability of the mighty Soviet nuclear empire.

We heard the calves wandering around, moaning, hungry and thirsty in the backyard. There would be no pasture for these creatures today. They had to suffer because their owners were mean Christian spies.

THEN AN OLD GERMAN gothic Bible was placed on the table. Mama jumped up, rushed to the table and put her hand on it.

"This was a gift from my mother!" she had tears welling up in her eyes. "It is an heirloom, the only thing I have from my mother. Please! Do not take it away!" Mama's parents and siblings, bar one sister, had died in concentration camps, were exiled or executed.

The muscles in the officer's cheeks tightened. He listed the Bible.

Mama said, "This will be a curse on you all! Do not take the Bible!"

Most of the people in our village belonged to the religion of Islam. Amazingly, when atheists persecute religious people, religious people of different faiths shaw empathy. On one side of this officer was a Kazakh, a Muslim. He did not like my mother's pronouncement of a curse and, looking nervously at the Russian, said:

"Hey, let us give it back. It is a bad omen, you know."

"No," the Russian insisted, "I understand you. We will return this book to you later, Ma'am."

Mama had spent many years in concentration labour camps and knew what the value of a promise from a communist officer was worth.

She stood at the table in front of the officers. Tears were running down her cheeks. Her hand was still on the Bible. Her eyes were searching around. She looked at me. We all were crying with her and wondering what she thought. For a while, she just stood, looked and cried. Then she moved away and sat down.

Later, she said that her initial instinct was to grab the Bible and run or throw it at me. She hoped that I would run and escape the officers. Then, I would hide the Bible somewhere, but she changed her mind, afraid something would go wrong.

In December, before Christmas, the court hearing spectacle began. It dragged on for several days. One by one, locals, neighbours, coworkers and church members were called to the witness stand. Some believers and locals gave positive and good testimony to the character of the three men and two women to be sentenced.

At Papa's sentencing, the state prosecutors quickly succeeded in persuading the judge and the jury that a real danger to the safety of the USSR existed. Papa was a spy, and they had found a radio /electrical-voltage-meter to prove it. The three "traitors" were sentenced under the criminal code: "A dangerous element in case of war." The state demanded 4-5 years imprisonment, but it was graciously reduced to three years, which they served in full.

Mrs. Uzolzeva was the state prosecutor. One day during the court proceedings, she was incredibly vicious and nasty when accusing the faithful. As she walked to her car, my uncle Jakob opened the door for her and said:

"Mrs. Usolzeva, can I ask you a question?"

"Yes. What do you want?" She squeezed out an unfriendly response.

"Do you love your job?"

She looked away and angrily slammed the car door. Uncle Jakob never got an answer.

On the last day, the arrested prisoners were led out through the back door, so no one had a chance to say goodbye. They locked all the doors so that no one could go outside the building and see the transporting truck. Mama ran over the stage to the door in the back that was just used to lead Papa out and was still open. She only saw the police truck peeling away with the prisoner. She would miss him for the next three years.

They would be taken away to prison and then transferred to a concentration labour camp. She looked around in distress and noticed Ivan, someone who had been to our house a lot and had been helped out by Papa many times, standing and watching her. He laughed mockingly aloud. He was one of the accusers. Mama just said, "A man with no conscience!"

The following Sunday, church service was depressing, sad, and filled with fervent prayers for the prisoners. It was heartbreaking to see those who had betrayed our Papa, accused him and cooperated with authorities sitting piously in church, praying and worshiping God.

"Why is he here?" I asked.

"He has a lot to repent for," Mama replied.

Depriving the church of its leaders caused a surge in ambitious young men to fill the gap. The persecutors, against their own wishes, had multiplied spiritual leadership in the church. For every prisoner, there were now ten younger, more vital and fearless preachers arising. It was said that some of the higher-ups in the government had been told that persecution was counterproductive. The Christians just multiplied even more.

The enemies of the truth are filled with blind rage. They cannot see. Those who experience the miracle of eyesight to see the actual reality will never remain atheistic. Enlightenment wakes you up. Sadly, most people are asleep. They are willing slaves forced to do evil by a much larger entity, an entity that they do not believe in.

CHAPTER 7
PROPHECIES OF THE FUTURE

- 1967 -

My favourite teacher Tatyana was reading from the works of Vladimir Ilyich Lenin, "It is true that liberty is precious; so precious that it must be carefully rationed." I think I was daydreaming in class. My thoughts swayed from the images of Papa in chains in prison to the raven croaking about something outside, to the beautiful face of my lovely teacher, to my neighbour Sergey who was trying to find something in his nose.

Tatyana was explaining the importance of the Ministry of Information. Boring! I know it already. Many houses have radios hanging on their outside walls. The Communist Party congress speakers would roar loudly for hours. The news could be summarized as praise of the socialist over-achievements, sports and weather. We received very little-to-no information about the awful Western world outside of the Warsaw Pact Countries. Journalists were free to say whatever the conformity required of them. People had different opinions, views and interests, but those who dared to express them paid a high price. The media tells government narratives. That's how they lied about Papa and our church. Our friends and neighbours were turned into enemies who ridiculed us. No one was really asking what was true.

The bell rang, and the school day was over. I was glad it was Friday, and there was no school for a couple of days. So, grabbing my bag, I headed out, but then I saw a mob of hooligans gathering in the school park under the odious statue of Lenin.

I went a long way home around to my cousin's Igor's house. My uncle and cousins did not go to church and lived a secular lifestyle. Our friendship was deteriorating. After the last year of persecutions and imprisonments, our town had emptied and was a little sadder and a little darker.

∽

CHRISTIANS WERE CALLED - People of the Book. We emphasize the importance of the Bible as a rule for life. We indeed do like literature, music, art and creativity. All of that originated with the Bible anyway! However, in a socialist regime, we were forced to develop our own sub-culture. Society did not want our contributions, views, opinions, lifestyle, or anything dear to us.

Our underground church viewed any "godless" media consumption, including books and movies, as a sin. In addition, entertainment such as dancing, singing secular songs or making "non-Christian" (whatever that means) music was also seen as harmful.

∽

SATURDAY WAS the day for our family's weekly bathing. We cleaned our Sunday dresses and did our house cleaning – a day of preparation for Church on Sunday. My older sister Lyda liked to listen to music on the radio and would turn it on.

Mama remarked, "Make sure you turn it off if visitors come!" In prison, Papa was still the Presbyter of our underground church, so we tried to guard his reputation.

Papa, like all of us, enjoyed reading. We had, despite pious peer pressure, a lot of books, newspapers and magazines at home. I remembered the day Papa had come home for lunch and shown Mama a pile of subscription slips. Mama gasped. He had spent a whole month's salary on subscriptions for newspapers like Pravda, Izvestia, Commsomolskaya Truth, and magazines like Crocodile (a humour magazine), Young Naturalist, Science and Religion, and Around the World, and so on. As kids, we loved it. Winter could come, and we would still have a great time.

Our attic was covered with a thick layer of old media prints, books, newspapers and magazines. It was absolutely a fire hazard but also a good insulator for those -40 Celsius winter weeks. We read and reread many classics that were translated into Russian. Alexandre Dumas' "The Count of Monte Cristo" and "The Three Musketeers," Howard Pyle's "The Merry Adventures of Robin Hood," a lot of pirate stories and sailing adventures, and of course, the Russian classics: Pushkin, Lermontov, Dostoyevsky, and Tolstoy.

One of our favourite pastimes was "Rakat", a self-made-up word from the Russian "raskasivat", meaning "telling a story". Sitting with friends in the hot and dusty attic of our house, on top of old papers and among drying apples and herbs, we would take turns fantasizing and creating fictional stories. It was a highly sophisticated art of weaving an impromptu novel. First, we would decide whose turn it was to be the lead storyteller. Then, we would pick a topic, for example, pirates, robbery, African adventure hunting, North American Cowboys and Indian tribes, etc. – it had to be exotic and take place in a faraway land that we knew we could never visit but had read or heard about. The lead storyteller would start, and then we would chip in our imaginary corrections. Rakat took us into a beautiful fantasy world far from reality, horror, suffering and real pain, and it made us heroes and mighty warriors. We would bring justice to the corrupt governments and greedy capitalists and snatch beautiful princesses from cruel and ugly old perverts. Every tiny detail had to be precisely described, and we would break out in screaming arguments about how the dress or weapon looked. Oh, how we desired the freedom to travel and see the wide exciting world, cultures, and nations and hear exotic languages like English, Arabic, or Spanish.

~

Two travelling men knocked at our door. Lyda opened it and asked them what they wanted. One asked in a very soft and over-exaggerated pious, quiet voice,

"Are the children of Abraham living here?"

"Not here," my sister told them, "continue on this road to the next crossing. The house on the left will be the home of Abraham and his children".

The men looked surprised but did not move. They knew that this was the home of the Presbyter, our Papa, and had used a secret code adopted by Christians to identify each other. My sister did not know about the code and had pointed them to our friend's house.

The misunderstanding was quickly sorted out, and the guests were welcomed inside. They stayed a few days and spoke extensively with the Christians who came in the evening and sat till late talking about secret church stuff in our living room.

At mealtimes, we sat all together at the table. As kids, we were not supposed to talk when grown-ups did, but we could listen. The adults were talking a lot about the future of the world and of prophecy.

"There will be a time when we will be free to travel the world and to openly believe in God and preach the Gospel of Jesus Christ," they would say. Their prophetic utterances were many and almost otherworldly. It sounded like the grown-ups were in their own fantasy world; they were playing "Rakat". We didn't believe it could ever happen. The mighty USSR could never crumble! Wasn't there a time coming when the whole world would become socialist and militantly atheistic with no room for Christianity?

That summer, our cousin Valentine, still a teenager, came for a visit. His family lived in the Siberian mining town where we had lived before. He was an earnest and very pious chap. He could recite whole books of the Bible by memory. Later in life, he became a well-known and respected evangelist in the vast Siberian Taiga and remote northern villages until his premature death in his forties. I feel honoured and humbled to have known Valentine and his sacrificial service for others in need.

"He is your example," the visitors would say to us. "Memorize and understand the scriptures. This discipline will serve you well at all times – in persecution, as we have it now, and in times of total freedom, as will come soon. When you are in prison and do not have books, your memory will be your library. When you are free to preach, you will be very skillful in presenting the truth to the ignorant and searching!"

This was a true prophecy! The USSR disintegrated in less than 20 years! In those days, it was inconceivable to imagine that the Soviet bloc countries would become the most open countries of the 21st century. The so-called "Western free countries" would willingly enslave themselves under socialist 'dictatorships.'

CHAPTER 8
FREE MEDICINE

Our town was comprised of 3,000 people, plus the surrounding counties of multiple hamlets. We had one medical doctor, Valery. He was a genius, a very talented and hard-working fellow. There was nothing on earth he could not fix and nothing in or on your body that he could not heal. He was assisted by nurses, but ultimately, he would call the shots. He would deliver a baby, then fix your teeth, then operate on someone's appendix, then place your broken foot in a cast, prescribe glasses, check your hearing, vaccinate, put someone in a coma, prevent your allergies and "cook" the hospital books. He was, without a doubt, the right person for our town. As a member of The Communist Party, his career was secure, and he couldn't make a mistake, even if he tried.

The only negative trait he had was his thirst. He was thirsty for a good drink and friends. Because of the respect and good fame he enjoyed, he received many gifts, and his booze collection was impressive. At the hospital, the nurses and staff learned to appreciate the exotic smell of all sorts of tasty spirits.

If a friend dropped by with an ailment, it was inexcusable not to celebrate it with a shot of the good stuff. A friend of his, Grigori, the tractor driver, went in with a rotten tooth. Valery had already healed a few friends and smelled happy. Out came another bottle, and down went the firewater.

"To disinfect," the doctor said.

Grigori, now feeling relaxed, stretched out in the dentist's chair.

"What tooth?" shouted Valery.

"This nasty sucker," Grigori said as he pointed to his mouth.

"No problem," said Valery, and he shoved his precision instrument into Grigori's mouth. There was a great pull, a mighty scream, and the nasty sucker was out.

Grigori spat out some blood, smiled and said, "Thank you." Then he shoved his dirty finger into the cavity, his smile dropped, and with a curse and many profanities, he explained that it was the wrong one. Valeri apologized. They had another shot of the calming drops, and Valeri pulled again, this time on the correct tooth. Grigori double-checked and, jumping out of the dentist's chair, shoved his sweaty face to the dentist's ear and, still spitting blood, screamed,

"Are you stupid?! Oy oy oy ... you left the bad one, again! Get back to work, you weirdo, and pull the right one this time!" Valery did as he promised, and this time he really did pull the right, nasty sucker out.

Friends are always friends, and after a few more shots and a philosophical analysis of the dental procedure, they parted. Valery ensured that Grigori was compensated with two magic potion bottles for the two innocent teeth killed.

I WENT to Mama to complain about my swelling cheek. Usually, we kids would go to Papa. He would take out his electrician's pliers, disinfect them on his working clothes, and relieve any tooth that bothered us. However, he was still in the labour prison camp. My rotten tooth became aggressive and had caused my cheek to swell up to the size of a soccer ball.

Mama worked a lot, as she was now the only provider for our large family. She looked and told me to go and see Valery, our versatile medical magician. The medical treatments are all free in the socialist system. I walked over to the clinic. Sitting at his desk, Valery asked, "What's up, my son?" I pointed to my face.

He looked and said, "Oy oy ... I will fix it, no problem." He led me to the dentist's room. After showing me the dentist's chair, he looked around for his instruments. Then, he turned to me with his big, shiny pliers and heavy alcoholic breath, and he said, "There is no point in anesthetics. The case is too far gone." With that, he placed the cold instrument of torture on my sensitive tooth, and before I could say "Oy!" it was out.

Valery looked again and said, "Oy, oy ... my son, there is a massive amount of pus. I will have to cut it open and disinfect the wound." He turned away to get his scalpel. A terror overcame me, and the only thought I had was: a blood infection! I do not want this drunk to cut anything that belongs to me! As a 12-year-old, I believed that this drunken, well-meaning medical professional would kill me. While he was facing his desk, I slipped down the chair and out of the room.

As I walked home, I was constantly sucking out the pus and spitting it on the dusty street. The blood mixed with yellow stuff seemed never-ending. However, by the time I reached home, it was just clean blood. So, I relaxed and walked into the kitchen. When Mama heard all the details, she simply said, "Well, don't eat anything for a few hours, now." Then, she gave me a tablespoon of vodka to rinse and disinfect my mouth. I spat the nasty stuff out and went outside and sat down in our backyard, trying to get the pain, tears, and shock under control. Sharick, our devoted canine, came and sat beside me and cheered me up.

Fall arrived, and we had our first snow. With the cold also came the annual flu season. Coughing, sore throats, headaches, and other symptoms arrived. At school, we also had the so-called spreading of germs. Valery, our doctor, was busy prescribing cough drops and other medications.

Mama was big on home remedies and did not trust the government experts. She worked in the hospital and knew what was going on. Mama's Opa Levin was a medical doctor in Tsar's Russia. Mama had probably inherited the doctor's bug, and she had a remedy for everything. When one of us complained about something, the prescription and medication were always ready. It varied between a lot of garlic, hot tea, a spoonful of vodka (a unique concoction of 750mg vodka and 1/3rd of the bottle filled with salt and pepper). After that, you would sweat the sickness out. It meant you dressed and lay in bed under five blankets and sweated. When your clothes and blankets were soaked through, you got up, changed and repeated. I resented the procedure with all my guts. I thought it was torture.

My brother Vania and I decided we needed toughening up, and Mama supported us. We got up regularly at 7 am to be in school at 8 am. When Mama woke us, we would run outside just in our undies, screaming, jump into the piles of snow and rub each other's chest and back with the snow. It was a constant nippy -25°C to -30°C. We did this almost every day through the winter. That winter, neither of us had a cold, and we were spared from swallowing the vodka-salt-pepper medication.

Regarding the vodka home remedy concoction – if someone is tempted to attempt something similar, I strongly suggest you don't try it at home. It was so awful and bitter that I hadn't been able to stand the smell of vodka my whole life. As far as I know, none of my siblings have been tempted by this poison either.

CHAPTER 9
C**OO**KED ECONOMICS

"Every cook should learn to govern the state," said Lenin in 1925. The "cook" that ran our town was Chairman Mogamedov. The mechanical garage in town was managed by his brother, Amir. His brother-in-law, Ura, operated the dairy processing plant. Other lucrative positions in our town were filled with his friends and relatives. Naturally, this was all done democratically and lawfully. A member of The Communist Party occupied every leadership position. No one could forge a serious career without a Communist Party membership ID. Then, to keep the place, you had to practice the chicken coop principle: "Fight with and spy on those who sit on your level and crap on those who are below you."

It was in the fall of 1967. The harvest time arrived, and it was as busy a time as ever. The whole town was bustling with activities. Siberian winters are cold and windy. What you did not prepare in the summer was hard to get in winter.

From our garden, we harvested a lot of veggies and some fruit. As a family, we did go out into the patches of forests and gather some wild berries and mushrooms. Papa and two neighbours had constructed a homemade tractor. Still, now Papa was almost a year in the prison labour camp. Our Christian neighbours came to help. In the open areas within forest patches around our town, they cut, dried and transported stacks of hay and straw to feed the cows in the winter. When the first frost would come, several men arrived to slaughter our pigs, geese and chickens. It was a gruesome and smelly occasion, but it gave us fat to cook and meat for the winter.

Mama and Lyda, with the help of the rest of us, preserved tomatoes, cucumbers, crabapples and cabbage in barrels for the winter.

A TABOR of travelling Gypsies arrived and pitched a tent camp outside our town. Colourful gypsy wagons formed a circle around the wondering city. Many beautiful horses were grazing around. At least this small community of the USSR empire seemed to live a free life and have no worries or problems. They sang, danced, they laughed and had, as it seemed to us, a great time all the time.

During the day, their women would go from home to home asking for food and money for their clairvoyance and palm reading services. Anxious girls, wives and mothers were eager to hear about their looming futures of misfortunes and misery. Statistically, no one believed in religious myths. Still, no one could prevent superstitious atheists from having a peek into the future.

Neighbours began to warn each other.

"Hey, sosed (neighbour). Hide everything – the caravans have arrived."

Gypsy kids would roam the streets and get into fights with us and take what was not hidden or nailed down. Babushka, at the edge of the town, complained that her dog had been stolen. It must have been the gypsies. They were blamed for everything.

Gypsy men practiced the free-market economy. They approached the town hall offices and offered their services. Our town's collective cattle barns as ever needed a lot of feed for the cows for the winter.

"We need hay," said the town clerk.

"How much hay? How much will you pay? We can provide as much as you need for your beautiful cows," said the gypsy baron to the clerk.

The local bureaucrats were constantly on the lookout to find a solution to bypass various ever-present dilemmas so that they could pocket more money from the collective budget for their own and their children's "exceptional" needs. Who could object to that?

Smelling an opportunity for another shortcut to save some rubles, a deal was struck after a short discussion. The contract was sealed with a handshake. All gypsy men, young and old, got to work. Everyone swung a scythe. They cut the grass in clearings between the patches of forest and in the fields. It dried, and then they gathered the land hay into big stacks. It was a lot – more, in fact, than the town needed. They also over-achieved on their promises and goals. The pay-out was in cash, as expected. Our esteemed chairmen also gave them a certificate of recognition for outstanding performance.

That same night the gypsies tossed the "certificate of outstanding performance" into their camp bonfire. There was loud singing and dancing till early morning. They broke up the tents that next day, packed their colourful wagons and beautiful horses, and left as if in a hurry. No one knew where they went, and they did not leave a forwarding address.

Boris, my Muslim neighbour, was my friend again and invited me to go to the Soviets' townhouse. Apparently, there was a celebration meeting.

"No one will let us in," I said.

"The chairman is my relative. We'll sneak in. They have a lot of food there, silly!"

This celebration was to mark the successful conclusion of another Five Year Plan, a balanced economic development, and the establishment of financial stability for our socialist collective farm.

The "more equals," or the educated elite and the bureaucrats, had their lavish party separate from the peasants in the Soviet townhouse. The food and decor, clothes and cars would be of a higher standard. Still, the program would actually be the same – vodka, moonshine, and lots of sarcasm and disrespect.

We met no problems when sneaking in. Boris said something in Kasakh, and the door opened. We grabbed some food and sat in the back corner. The room was large, and the air was thick with alcohol, music, and cigarette smoke fumes.

The esteemed Chairmen Magomedov got up in the middle of an already quite boozy party and shouted in a drunken delirium:

"Comrades! We are all comrades, but amongst us are some comrades who are not our comrades! We recognize only those comrades that are true comrades," He paused, catching his breath. His word choice was of the highest poetic value.

"Now! We have received three gramophones! Glory to our Holy Communist Party! As a thank you for our-no, your hard work, Comrades, and for the overproduction of grain, cattle, potatoes, tomatoes, milk ... and something else, what was it... ..."

Raising his glass of moonshine, he spilled a little on his mistress to his left. He looked right at his wife, guiltily, and bellowed,

"Glory to the Soviet Government!!! Now, comrades! For all these great achievements and sacrifices, I would like to give you recognition. All of you have done an excellent job! You worked very, very hard!"

Applause and laughter. The overfed and lazy bureaucrats had no idea what work was, but they liked the positivity.

"Now, the highest prize is a gramophone! One gramophone is awarded to my brother-in-law Ura, the best ever for milk and butter production! You all benefited from his generous gifts. Right? Applause, please! Thank you. Thank you ... Ura: you had a hard year with those good-for-nothing bozos."

Applause and laughter again.

"The second gramophone goes to my brother Amir. He is the excellent administrator of the mechanical ... the garage. His heroic service to building socialism is a great example to everyone! Applause, please! Louder ... Don't be so shy!!!!

If you need to borrow a truck or repair your Lada, where do you go? Ahhhh ... to Amir!

There you go. I knew that you would all be pleased. And the third gramophone is for the one and only, the best chairmen of our Oblast, hahaha! and that is, of course, me!!!"

There was wild applause and a burst of drunken, jealous laughter.

"Now, who here votes against the decisions of The Communist Party?! Anyone?... No? Great! So it is unanimously decided. Thank you all."

We had enough of this and sneaked out and went home.

EVERYONE IN TOWN received the same minimal universal salary. Only people with connections to the "higher powers" were more equal than others and had slightly higher pay. No one was unemployed. And yet, everyone was worried about how to survive the upcoming winter.

The winter arrived. We settled into going to school, looking after the cattle in our small barn and reading books. The wind on bitterly cold nights had a unique sound that brought the sensation of loneliness and sadness.

In February, when the winter was most severe and the numerous herds of cattle were stuck in collective barns, they needed their fodder. The workers went out to the fields to bring in the "gypsy" hay. They reached the first stack, drove the tractor-fork into the pile and tried to lift it. The tractor stalled. What was going on? They tried again. Nothing! By hand, they uncovered a big bush! Those charlatans, the gypsies, had just covered bushes with hay! They went to the next and the next. All were the same. Big brushes and shrubs were covered with as little hay as possible. It looked impressive, but it was simply a clever scam.

There was another economic crisis. The Town Council had a series of meetings to find someone to blame, but the cattle were still hungry! So, after a couple of lower-ranked clerks were accused and demoted, the town council unanimously passed another stimulus package. More money needed to be spent. In our progressive socialist town, everything cost twice over. The town had to buy hay from our neighbouring collective farms and pay the topped-up costs. Stressed-out bureaucrats were handsomely compensated and sent to luxury resorts to recover. Well researched reports were sent to the Republic Agricultural Ministry that stated, "The culprits of this shameful, anti-socialistic scam have been caught and mercilessly punished." The peaceful routine was again established.

The townsfolk said, "Oh, well!"

CHAPTER 10
ESSENTIAL RITUALS

My cousin Victor was in the navy. He was my hero, and when he returned from his compulsory service, he gave me his marine Navy jacket. My oldest sister Lyda was an excellent seamstress and altered it to my size. Now, as a 12-year-old, I strolled through town as a dazzling Navy seaman.

One day, I overheard Victor telling Mama that a group of shops where he worked as a property manager were looking for a night security guard. Papa was in prison, and Mama alone made life possible for all of us. She worked in the kitchen of the hospital. My older brother Yasha was away in military service. Lyda was doing most tasks related to the running of our home. Then it was me, "the man." After me, there were my younger siblings Adina, Vania and Anna.

I felt like I needed to take charge of the situation, and I believed I had found a solution. Knowing that body language and appearance were essential, I put on my navy uniform and went to apply for the job. I found the woman responsible in the HR department and told her that I was the man they were looking for. I could do the night shifts, securing their buildings if they paid me a decent salary.

I believed my negotiations would have ended in a victory if Victor had not accidentally passed by and seen me in the office. He stormed in, apologized to the lady and forced me out and told me to go home. Then, he described everything to Mama. They both laughed, which really hurt my masculine feelings. I was convinced that I could have landed the best job in town with my appearance and assertiveness if only the adults hadn't messed it up.

As understanding and wise as she always was, Mama told me to concentrate on my schoolwork. I would work for money plenty enough in my lifetime, but not at that time. She healed my "emotional wounds" by telling me that the HR department lady said she was very impressed by my persona and would hire me any time – after I'd finished school.

"Body Language, including dress, facial expressions, posture, gestures and hand movements, are all very important," the youth leader told us many times. "It is just as vital as the words we speak. It is something we don't think about when we're talking. Praying is having a private audience with God. We pray standing or kneeling or laying on our faces and never sitting! It is disrespectful. You would never talk to a socialist bureaucrat whilst sitting. Would you? How much more important is God than one of these men."

It was often repetitive and over the top; no one needed to explain it to us – we never prayed sitting! Our Christian traditions were strong, and we did love our rules.

When Christians travelled and had to eat in public canteens, they would always stand to pray before the meal. Other people's ridiculing remarks did nothing to deter them from doing what was right.

As Papa and the other two men from our church arrived in their concentration camp, they continued to live by their Christian traditions. At their first time in the meal hall, the three stood up and thanked God for the food. The inmates had never seen such an open display of religion. All hell broke loose as laughter, screams, curses, and insults filled the air. Then, as food and other objects started flying at them, suddenly someone shouted,

"Stop and cease!"

Immediately the noise cut out, and everyone quickly concentrated hard on their fodder. The authoritative voice belonged to a man who sat at the head of a separate table. He was surrounded by what looked like a small personal guard of fairly large and muscular warriors. He was also a convict, but he commanded enormous authority.

"Let those men pray! If anyone bothers them, he will have a problem with me!" He kept his domineering and despising gaze on the inmates for a while. An impressive royalty, he was the Thief-in-Law. To the rest of the world, it was synonymous with a "Godfather." To be crowned as such, you had to earn it: you had to live according to the "Understanding" of the NGO (Non-Government Organization), display leadership skills, and have an impressive and verifiable criminal record. A council of other Thief-in-Laws would conduct the coronation and induct you into the "Hall of Infamy," presenting you to the world as the new "Thief-in-Law." Knees were tattooed with stars or crosses, in addition to other tattoos telling the histories of your accomplishments. You lived by a codex: you never worked or held a job, you did not have a family, you never knelt before any human (police, government, other criminals, nobody, never ever). God and women were exempt. Breaking the codex meant torture and painful death.

That night his warriors called Papa and the other Christians to an audience with the boss.

"Do you know why I ordered those stupid fools to shut up in the feeding hole?" he asked benevolently.

"Yes," they answered, "because God ordered you to do so!"

The Thief-in-Law did not expect such a response and was speechless for a second.

"DID you hear that?!" he suddenly shouted, delighted by such an eye-opening revelation.

"I am assisting God! God Himself instructed me! I am fulfilling God's plans!" He was elated by the fantastic insight. He pointed with his finger to the guards and his subjects and continued:

"Get it into your brainless skulls! God! The Almighty! God Himself is ordering my life!" He stood up, stretched, making himself as tall as he could. He seemed very self-righteous at that moment. The only thing that was missing was a halo above his head.

"No one will ever bother you; you can pray as much as you want," the "Emperor" granted. He tried to sound as charming as he could muster. "If any of those cons try to stop you, tell us, and we will secure your freedom!" he assured. Papa and the other Christians were never bothered again.

The self-proclaimed socialistic democratic government took away the freedom to pray and imprisoned the pastors for doing so. The lawless criminals reinstated their liberty to pray to God and ensured others respected that.

SOCIAL EVENTS WERE ORGANIZED for the prisoners from time to time: concerts, singers, musicians, and political lectures. On one memorable occasion, a magician was invited, described as a trickster and charmer of ghosts. As usual, attendance was compulsory for all. The charmer began his presentation with a grand speech that promised the "best show ever." After a few initial attempts, he could not fulfil any of his promises. He was visibly embarrassed and frustrated. The convicts started to ridicule and insult the poor performer. Then, he stopped and looked intently into the faces of the prisoners. He went row by row. Trying to catch the prisoners' eyes, he stopped at the few Christians sitting at the back together.

"You, over there. Get out of here immediately! You are the problem! I cannot do anything! Different spirits. Who are you? Get them out of here!" he shouted.

Papa and fellow Christians left. The magic was restored, and the fun could begin. All his tricks ran smoothly, and the crowds cheered the magician and his masterful performances.

THE CAMP WAS DIVIDED into two zones: the working zone and the living zone. Every morning the prisoners were lined up, the soldiers did a roll call. The prisoners were counted and searched before they crossed over into the working zone. In the evening, it was a reverse procedure. Coming back, they searched them more thoroughly. Guards were wary that someone could manufacture and smuggle a weapon into the living zone. But the 18-20-year-old inexperienced soldiers were no match for the seasoned and sophisticated criminals. Things travelled and arrived where they had to go.

Prison camp life runs in a relatively orderly fashion. There was one crowned Thief-in-Law presiding over it. With the arrival of another crowned mobster, the hierarchy had to be sorted out. Everything needed to be proper according to the codex of the NGO law and order. If plan "A" negotiations were unsuccessful, plan "B" was assassinations. If that failed, full-fledged combat would break out. In this instance, the guards locked down the camp completely. There were no services; no one went in or out. Anyone who tried to climb the barbwire to escape the horror of a gang war would be shot by the guards. After a week or so of conflict, a clear winner would emerge, and the disruption would die down. Cleaners and guards then moved in and removed the dead, and transported the injured to the hospital. Someone would be found and declared guilty as a scapegoat, and a trial would be staged. With a topped-up sentence, the "guilty" party would be dispatched to a separate prison camp.

All that week, Papa, and other prisoners, hid under the bunk beds or in closets. Staying hungry but alive was the prerogative. They waited out the emergence of a new or affirmation of the old Thief-in-Law.

During those three years of imprisonment, the psychological experts played many mind games on the Christians. The goal was to change their minds – a re-programming of a sort. If a believer caved in, compromised, denied his faith in Christ, promised to be an informer, or succumbed to offers of partying and sensual pleasure, he was guaranteed freedom. He was pardoned, released from prison and went home. If he did not, the threats and terror would continue.

"Do you not care about your wife and six children? Don't you realize how hard it is for her to manage life without you?" the KGB officer asked Papa empathetically.

"You know it well that just by signing this pledge, you will be released by tomorrow, and you could go home-sweet-home to your wife and children? Do you love them?"

"Warm fireplace, home meals, playing with your kids ... do you love them?"

"Oh, your wife probably has a lover? That's why you do not want to go home! Aren't you jealous?"

"Listen, we do not demand anything draconically impossible. It is all straightforward. We want you to obey your biblical convictions and submit to the government, as the apostle Paul commanded you in Romans 13! That's all!"

"You see, in that sense, you should take the Bible literally! The other, contradictory views should be kept to yourself.

"You will be pardoned. You do not have to abandon your personal beliefs! Oh, no, you can believe in the four walls, in the privacy of your home, but do not dare to speak of God and Christian values in the marketplace or to other people. Do not proselytize. Do not convert others to Christianity, and have some respect and tolerance. In no circumstance should you ever teach children religion! These are backward, primitive, unscientific and anti-social ideas."

"So, what do you say?"

"I cannot deny my faith, and I will not change my Christian traditions," Papa answered.

"Well, then, stupid, rot in this rat-infested place all your life. Idiot!" The officer summed up the meeting.

These meetings and reviews happened regularly, a couple of times a year. The integrity and character of believers were secretly admired but dutifully attacked in the public eye. Those who resisted the propaganda machine of socialist indoctrination and dared to think critically and independently were ridiculed, marginalized, imprisoned, and even killed. It did not matter if you were religious or not, if you dared to look outside of the socialistic box or criticized the government line, you were a cockroach, and you would be squashed.

CHAPTER II
CONCENTRATION CAMP HOLIDAYS

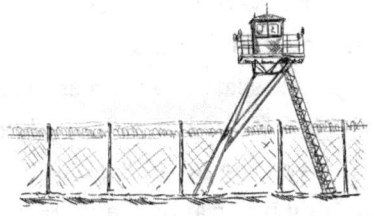

- 1968 -

Papa spent a total of nine years in Soviet prisons and concentration camps. When I was ten years old, he was incarcerated for the second time for three years. As described in chapter six, he was the founding presbyter of our underground church. To visit him in prison was always exciting. A lot of families in the USSR had a relative or a friend imprisoned. At times, 10 percent of the population was in prison labour camps as cheap labourers' resources building-specific governmental projects. So, visiting a prisoner was not that extraordinary. And yet, Mama could see him only a few times a year. Once a year, she would take some of us kids with her. If permitted, we would go inside the concentration camp into a separate, barbed-wired, high-fenced area. Guards on towers with machine guns would be our view from the windows. We would occupy a single-room cell as a family for a max of three days. We could go out and shop and bring some extra clothes and food to the room. Papa still had to go and work 8 hours each day, but he would spend the nights with us.

The 190 km route required a whole day bus ride to Pavlodar, where the camp was located. The buses were slow, small and loud. In the winter, the driver would let the exhaust pipe run inside the length of the bus; this was the heating system.

We never stayed in hotels. Honestly, I did not even know they existed. Christian hospitality was practiced generously, and we always stayed at an old couple's house – a typical Russian structure with blue window shutters.

Titovich and Ivanovna were members of the local underground church. They were the most loving and hospitable people I had ever known. They shared their scarce resources with us generously. A small government pension did not permit any luxuries. However, the grandma cooked and served the tastiest meals.

I grew up not knowing my grandparents from either side. Stalin's socialistic, benevolent dictatorship had resulted in both my grandfathers' imprisonment and firing squads executing both. My grandmothers died before I could know them. Anyone old and friendly triggered in me a fondness, and I graciously endowed them with the honourable title of "grandma and grandpa."

Early the next day, we would catch a city bus to the "Zone." Then, we would sit in the small building outside the labour camp, sometimes for a day, sometimes for a few days, waiting for permission. The prison management would make spontaneous decisions about who was allowed to visit. The others had to wait another day or two.

AFTER A WHOLE DAY'S WAIT, we did not get permission to see Papa. We took a city bus back to the old couple. We reached the gate of their wooden house late at night. We banged the wooden gate as loud as we could. Titovich, with a smile, greeted us,

"In the Name of God, please come in, come in! Don't be shy. Ivanovna prepared food for you. It's getting cold. We were waiting and praying for you."

In the cold and harsh reality, it felt so good. Then, Titovitch would take his old, worn bible, always placed on the kitchen table, and read us something. He would say the most comforting and assuring prayers. His deep faith in a good God filled the room with warmth and coziness. I loved him; he was my Opa (grandfather).

While the adults were talking, we ate and fell asleep at the table. Mama was a tough woman, but sometimes she wept. She and Papa were 43 years old then and had six children.

The next day, we took another bus ride to the prison labour camp and once again waited for an officer to stop and call our family name. Some prisoners had their sentences diminished and would leave the camp during the day, usually to perform errands. They liked to stop on the way in or out of the camp at the cabin where the prisoners' wives were waiting. They would come in and flirt with the women. One asked Mama,

"What is the name of your sek?" (A Russian slang for a prisoner.)

"Ivanovitch," my mother said.

He laughed and said, "Oh, that old guy with a bald head! Look, I am much better looking. Leave him and come with me."

"He is bald, but he is mine," replied Mama, smiling.

I was proud of Mama's quick-wittedness.

In his twenties, Papa had worked in the coal mines in Siberia. He had a hair loss problem. Someone suggested he shave it all off to stimulate growth. I don't know what he shaved his head with, but the hair took it personally and never returned. He was bald for as long as I remembered him.

Finally, an officer called our name, and the entry routine

commenced. Several iron gates opened and closed before and behind us. The first station was where the soldiers looked over our documents and asked for our names. The next station was where we had to show what we were bringing in. We had a loaf of bread, a piece of cheese, sausage, a package of candy, tea and some other provisions. The officer took out his bayonet and poked and cut to reveal whether something was hidden inside. In the end, everything was messed up and in crumbs, but we could take it in.

Smuggling money, drugs, cigarettes, and other valuables for the prison camp's black market was a big business. Christians sometimes baked a small portion of the bible into a loaf of bread. One of our friends spent 14 years in the gulags had his wife send him some rubles. The 10, 20 and 50 ruble bills had a picture of Lenin on them. So he rolled the bills up into small money-balls and swallowed them. Later, in prison, he visited the toilet and pressed the money out.

"The only problem," he said, was that "Lenin didn't like it and came out looking a little pale." he laughed.

We spent a few days with Papa. The only thing I remember is that we sat at the table and ate. Papa smiled a lot. Mama was happy. The room was very dark and gloomy. The one window had heavy iron bars and offered a view of a soldier standing on the tower, smoking and holding an AK47. I was 12 years old.

CHAPTER 12
FOR FILTHY LUCRE'S SAKE I

Igor, my cousin, and Sasha, his friend, met me in the backstreet.

"Do you want to do some good and help an old, sick man? He pays," said Igor.

"Sure," I said.

We went to a rundown dwelling. The windows were covered, and it was dark and grimy inside. The frail old man, Simul, spent his days in bed. We did not know what ailed him, but he was chronically thirsty for a strong drink. So, my friends did daily runs to top up his continually decreasing liquor collection. Then, they took the empty bottles to recycle and made some extra bucks.

Simul was a perfect example of a socialist male. Socialism, which was popularized by Karl Marx, is an attractive-sounding hell. Karl was a passive drunk whose most essential skills were a mastery of words, poetry, and manipulating others. Marx's explicit personality traits can be observed in all of his disciples: laziness, confusion, violence, disrespect toward family and parents, neglecting your own children, misusing other people for personal gain, envying others' success, having no idea how money worked (despite his widely distributed book on "Das Kapital"), racism against Jews, and fascination with destruction and the "Prince of Darkness."

Simul was living out Karl Marx's ideals. His wife and children had to move out, and they found a home in a small mud-house close by. I knew the family. They all were fine Christians and belonged to our church. Their daughter was the one I had my eyes on.

Now, I got to know my potential father-in-law. He ignored God and neglected his family and his health. He did not look happy, but he also had no time to think because booze took all the time of the day. He could buy our services as street boys and be a boss while telling us what to do.

It was in stark contrast to my family. Mama, and our older sister Lyda, made sure that it was always clean, fresh, that it smelled good, there was tasty food on the table and a lot of light and sunshine. This old goat lives alone in hell, I thought with pity. Soon, he'll be dead and then he'll go to absolute hell! No bright and glorious future of communism for this one!

"Who's the new guy?" asked Simul. His face was swollen, unshaved, and crowned with frazzled hair.

"My cousin, Heyna," said Igor.

"Ah, the preacher's son. How is your dad enjoying his holiday in jail?" he chuckled.

I did not like him already. Then, we went to do some cleaning in the house. Honestly, we did not know what we were doing, and I believe we left the place unchanged, but the old man gave us some money. Before we went outside, Simul called to Sasha and whispered something in his ear. Then we left. While walking out onto the street, Sasha was quiet and clearly thinking about something.

The next day Igor was at my place early.

"The old man gave Sasha money to return to someone he owes. It is a lot," he said.

"How much?"

"Well, I think it's 75 rubles."

The average monthly salary of a worker was about 60 rubles. We looked at each other. It was a lot of money!

"Sasha and I decided to steal it. The old goat will forget whom he gave what, anyway. So we hid it in the back of Sasha's family's cow barn," he said. "Now, I'll go and talk to Sasha while you go and dig out the money."

"It's stealing! I can't do that!" I retorted.

"Are you stupid? Sasha and I stole the money. You are just helping to pass it on. It is a money transfer. It's very different to stealing," Igor was very persuasive.

I was worried that I would provoke the Great Spirit to anger. That had happened the last time we stole the single-barrel shotgun. I had promised to never steal again, but this transaction made sense.

OUR PLAN SUCCEEDED, and we successfully transferred money from the evil criminals to us, the innocent souls. We divided the booty 50/50. I suddenly had more money than I'd ever had in my life.

Now I could afford things I had always wanted. Pretending to be a generous mobster, I invited a few friends, and we went shopping. We actually only bought two things, cigarettes and chocolate waffles. I loved these waffles. Mama bought them rarely, and then they had to be divided among all my siblings. Cigarettes? Well, everybody smoked. Smoking was cool. I wanted to try it out.

Standing behind a high fence, we felt safe and were dividing cigarettes and waffles among us. Suddenly, we all heard God's voice from heaven, "Boys, what are you doing?" It was so surprising that "our hearts slipped into our rears," as the Russian proverb goes. We looked up. There, on the 10-meter-high fence, was our church youth leader enjoying the view. We murmured an excuse and took off.

Under our great Idol Lenin statue, we ate a vast amount of

chocolate waffles in the park. Then, I tried to smoke for the first time. It was awful, and I got very sick and dizzy. Vomiting and rolling on the grass, I hated everyone and every decision I had made. It was so utterly repulsive and idiotic that for the rest of my life, I would never smoke. Actually, three things have held no attraction for me my whole life: smoking, vodka (this was liberally mixed with salt and pepper as Mama's potent all-ailments antidote), and chocolate waffles.

Carelessly, I made it home, but my trouble was just beginning. Mama, with one glance, recognized that something was wrong.

"Heyna, you look so pale! Why do you smell of cigarettes?" she asked, worried. Even at this young age, I had learned that there are two to whom you cannot lie: God and your Mama. Somehow, they always know the truth. Later in life, I had to add: God, Mama and Wife, as there is no point in having secrets from this trinity.

Through tears, I told the whole truth and showed the still substantial amount of money left. Mama was very sad, and I felt so awful and guilty.

She said, "In our family, we do not steal! You do not take what you did not work or pay for. You know that!"

"Every vice originated from a misuse of a good thing," she continued, "but smoking has no benefits for humans whatsoever. Smoking is just incense for the demons! That's how stupid it is."

Mama returned the money to Simul and apologized for her criminal son. It must have been very upsetting for her. Her husband was in prison for being a church leader, and now her son was a criminal.

I was grounded, so I sat on the ground in our front yard. Sharik sat beside me. I started to cry, realizing that the dog was a better person than me. He guarded our house against thieves, but now I was one. Now I knew it was not just that I could be bad. I was bad! I lied, stole, cheated, hurt others, fought ... the list of my transgressions was growing. Stealing was more straightforward the second time. Your conscience is made of rubber; you can stretch and mould it. A good excuse can silence it very effectively. However, there is an evolution! Like everyone else, I would evolve in one direction or in the other. I could have become like Simul, an old socialist goat living in hell, or an honest, admirable Christian man like Papa, who was imprisoned but destined for heaven.

---

[1] Titus 1:11 the KJ Bible

CHAPTER 13
ABDIEL, THE SLAVE

"If you do not believe in the evil in man, you will never appreciate the goodness of God!"

So said the smiling old man, his steel tooth glittering in the sun. We called him just "The Slave." We did not know where he came from or where he lived. He appeared unexpectedly, conducted communion services, prayed for the sick, encouraged the fearful, helped resolve issues and then he would leave. He literally walked out of town.

He was not a great orator, but he knew the Bible by heart. He was the kind of person who, at first sight, didn't stand out. He appeared to be nothing special and indeed not a TV personality. He walked with a limp and was a little chubby. His health and body were battered by decades of imprisonment and exile in the Siberian gulags.

I would sit with the rest of our youth group and listen to him speak. He was the father figure I was missing.

"To find your own life, you have to lose it. Be humble and admit that you cannot understand yourself, or the meaning of your life, or the purpose for your existence, or answers to so many other puzzling life questions," Abdiel said.

"A human, despite education and meditation, will never find the blueprint for life. We don't have brains for that!" He lifted his gnarled finger to make an important point.

" You have to purposefully lose your life for the sake and goals of God. Dedicate your life to His mission. God is then He who will come to look for you, find you and give you the abundance of life. The bliss of being found by God is the highest joy and fulfilment that a human can ever experience."

"Those who try to find themselves and the meaning for their own petty, private lives, all by themselves, will, in the end, lose everything."

We looked up to our guru and lapped up his words. Naturally, the meaning of a lot of his philosophies came to light later in my life.

When you spent a little time with him, you realized that you had the privilege of being in the presence of a real saint. He called himself "The Slave of the Almighty." He did not pray; he conversed with God as with an old friend. The spiritual world was not just "somewhere out there"; it was here, right where he stood – he was a very original and surreal individual.

At the beginning of the 1960s and 70s, persecution intensified, and thousands of church leaders were incarcerated. Abdiel became God's vagabond, a travelling preacher, a saint that brought sanity to the insane world. Many small Christian house churches, comprised of intimidated and fearful believers, would pray and hope that this Slave of God would visit them. He provided hope in suffering and dignity in discrimination.

ABDIEL LIVED AN ELEMENTARY LIFE. Having no car or other means of transportation, he travelled by hitchhiking. He covered all of Pavlodar Oblast (Province), an area of a small country or as big as

Greece. He was a soothing "Voice of God" in the ever-present madness. We admired his disregard for government restrictions and bullying.

He prayed before doing anything. Some of the locals would accompany him for a while on the highway. They often wondered that he never raised his hand to stop any cars or trucks. He would say,

"The car that God sends for me will stop."

He would walk until a car stopped. He believed that the driver was then the person sent by God and needed to hear the Truth.

Once on a bitter, freezing and windy winter day, no one would stop. The walkers all started to freeze. Then, in the distance, they saw a truck standing still. Abdiel said,

"See, there is already someone waiting for us."

The driver lifted the hood and looked for the engine problem – it would not start. "The Slave" slowly strolled up to him and said, "Young man, close the hood and start the truck; I am coming with you."

"You *&%$#@! Old man, what do you know about trucks? Go away!" This was the polite response.

"I said, close the hood and start the truck!" demanded the Slave.

The driver reluctantly got into the truck and cranked the starter. The engine sprang happily to life. He looked surprised and invited the old man to take the passenger seat.

"Who are you?" he asked, a little nervous. Most people are outwardly atheists but inwardly very superstitious.

"My son, God wanted you to give me a ride," answered the saint. For the rest of the trip, Abdiel had a captive audience of one. As always, he provided an engaging conversation, explaining that Jesus Christ was the Saviour of the world, and He loved the driver's lost soul, also.

ONE WEEKEND there was a secret meeting of regional pastors. It happened before Papa was imprisoned. Church leaders met in a private house, closing the window shutters to reduce the chance of being discovered by a KGB snitch. They would talk and pray for a few days and nights. Then, they would sleep on the long bus ride home and continue working their regular jobs on Monday morning while hoping no one noticed and no one reported them to frustrated and miserable bureaucrats.

In one of the exchanges, Papa expressed his frustration with a local bureaucrat. He had become increasingly aggressive towards the believers.

Papa said, "So, I prayed that God would punish him. God should stop him!"

Abdiel replied, "Oh, Brother, this is no good. God might do exactly that. God hears even our prayers to curse someone. You will have someone's life on your conscience."

"Once," he continued, "a zealous KGB threatened me with arrest and imprisonment. I got angry. Then I prayed. The man had a stroke. He never recovered, lost his lucrative post, and ended his life in poverty. I sinned twice: I got angry, and I cursed a man. I vowed never to do it again. We should simply bless those who persecute us, as our Lord taught us."

At that meeting, there was a man who was dying from liver disease. He asked for prayers. Abdiel said to all the pastors present, "Those of you who have doubts that this man will be healed today, please leave the room."

There was an awkward silence. It was kind of embarrassing for men of faith to show their lack of faith. Then one pastor left, and another. In the end, all left except three and the sick. Papa was one of those that stayed.

The Slave said to the ill man, "Confess all your sins. Do not leave anything out. If you do not confess honestly and remain silent on some, you will be healed today anyway, but the problems will come back with a vengeance. It will be worse with you the second time."

The man confessed honestly all he knew and could remember. He took some time, but no one was rushing him. Then they laid their hands on him and prayed a simple prayer. The pain left, and the man did not have any problems for the rest of his life.

"Prayer in the name of Jesus Christ has enormous power to heal and change reality, but it has to be spoken in faith, with no doubts. Confess your sins and your past service to the demons. The sickness and problems will never return," he taught the astounded pastors.

ONE DAY he said to his wife, "I need to visit a church." She tried to convince him not to go. It was bitterly cold and late in the evening. He said, "I will go to the highway and see if God sends me transportation. If not, I will come home."

He left. After an hour, he was back. No one had picked him up. He washed and went to his bedroom. His wife watched him undress, kneel down, raise his hands and declare, "God is Almighty!"

She went to another room and continued stitching. Then, she got up, went back and saw Abdiel lying in bed, head covered with a blanket. "Good," she thought, "he is asleep." Then something bothered her; she went back again, approached the bed and lifted the cover. He was gone. "He changed his address of residence," cried his wife of 65 years.

The Slave, Abdiel, had gone to be with the Lord he so faithfully served.

Many believers travelled to attend his funeral. The KGB and militia watched and even made sure the long procession with music and speeches was peaceful. They would not usually allow such a big gathering and parade. It looked like a famous celebrity was carried to rest. The small town had never seen so many people, speeches, processions or a music band. But, when curious onlookers asked who died, the KGB officers repeated again and again,

"Yes, a very influential Servant of God has died."

CHAPTER 14
DEATH OF A CHURCH

- 1969 -

An underground church whose leaders are incarcerated would get plenty of visits from well-meaning itinerant preachers. A man by the name of Joseph came to our town in the Fall. He was from the warm, exotic region on the Black Sea. When he arrived, the rain changed to snow, and the ground froze over.

He was a distant relative of some of our church members. This fifty-something-year-old charmer was a slim, almost 6-foot tall man with intense deep eyes, a beak-like nose supported by a square moustache and was crowned with a chop of black hair combed to one side. He spoke in a high-pitched, pious yet nervous voice and was constantly adjusting his round spectacles.

He enjoyed the honour of being the only preacher for several weeks – a stark departure from our customary three sermons. Commanding respect and often interrupting others, he was a fast talker and used many unfamiliar words.

I was extremely bored by his complicated monologues. Still,

being well trained to respect my elders, especially those who preach, I patiently endured this indulgence.

Somehow, he disregarded that men had to work hard all day long and were exhausted. He still demanded that they come to listen to his teachings every evening. He said women did not need to come.

He had a big story to tell. He claimed to have been elected by God to receive exclusive revelations. Having an intimate understanding of future things to come, he unveiled his wise survival plans. He quickly gained a large following. The new prophecies he spoke of were spellbinding and fascinating.

Joseph made people feel guilty for still believing the historical classical Christian doctrines.

"If you suffer," he said, "it is entirely your own fault." He rationally dismantled what he called out-of-fashion, harmful, offensive and untrustworthy theology. He presented, as he explained, a more sympathetic, modern, progressive and profound humanistic concept of Hell and Heaven. He claimed to have heard from God personally, so no one dared to contradict.

We began to shift into two classes of Christians: those in the know (the more spiritual) and those who didn't get it.

Then, he travelled to the city of Pavlodar and visited the prisoners in the labour camp. His cousin, Papa and the Carpenter were the three prisoners from our town. The man we called The Carpenter was the father of the youth leader in our church, and I've never understood why he, and not his son, was imprisoned. After a day, his imprisoned cousin was also converted to brand new teachings. As a triumphant guru satisfied with his achievements, Joseph returned back home. I actually never heard of him again, but the seeds he planted found fertile ground. This time the church was tainted from the inside.

Papa was released in December 1969, and all the prisoners returned home. The church had an enthusiastic reunion to celebrate, but the joy was short-lived. The new dogmas had taken root already and had begun to blossom.

The new doctrines began to be discussed in our Wednesday Bible study meetings. Papa started to publicly correct the unusual ideas and philosophies. He quickly discovered that almost all were infected with these new revelations.

Nightlong discussions ensued, and disagreements heated up, spilling over into disrespect. It would take multiple chapters to go into the theological details here that caused the division. But what happens when you are the leader and alone on one side of the argument? The majority rules. The church council of brothers united and excommunicated my Papa, his family and relatives from the church. All were accused of inciting division and heresy. Excommunication from the church is equal to damnation to hell. Belonging to the church, the bride of Jesus Christ is the only ticket to heaven. Outside of the church, there is no salvation.

They had damned to hell the founder and the presbyter of their church. The man who had just experienced persecution risked his life, sacrificed his family and freedom, and spent three years in a labour camp for preaching the gospel. The reason? He was disrespectful to Joseph, the guru. The preacher of a new doctrine. A hijacker of the church.

The underground church movement was very well organized and had regional Über-Pastors who oversaw the unity and guarded against heresy. For our Siberian region, a man named Korney was that authority. There were no phones or internet, so it took a few weeks for a letter about our church troubles to arrive. He came to inquire. He listened to all parties for several days. Then he called the church together. Korney stated that the new revelations were not new and weren't a revelation. It was an old practice of choosing and picking what you liked on a religious smorgasbord and making up your own brand of Christianity. Christian, occult, and other world religions were mixed together and spiced up with finesse, ego, and pride. If the church stuck to these teachings, the whole church would be expelled from the country-wide union of underground churches and declared obstinate.

The board of elders gave in, and the church accepted Korney's recommendations. We, as a family and our relatives, were welcomed back into the church family. Papa was reinstated as the leader, but emotions are a more powerful force than reason. Nothing would ever be as it was. Relationships, trust and friendships were ruined. One after another, Christian families left town. After a few years, the church shrank to zero. The sinister goal had been achieved; at last, the church dissolved. It was not the persecution, fines, discriminations or abuses that destroyed the church; it was the quarrel among brothers. The town was left to people who were indifferent, godless and desperate drunks.

Our family was one of the last to leave town. Only a few praying babushkas remained. Years later, the townspeople commented, "When the Baptists left town, God lifted His blessing. We became cursed. Weather and nature turned against us. The fields did not produce bountiful harvests anymore. People become demoralized. Crime and alcohol problems did the rest."

Buildings fell into disrepair. Businesses closed. Today there is almost nothing left: ruins, empty streets and the occasional horse buggy. Stray dogs, wild animals and feral cats feel at home now, though.

CHAPTER 15
BECOMING A CHRISTIAN

- 1971 -

When I was 15, my view of the world became crystal clear: socialists were atheists, Christians were not socialists. All those who denied God would eventually become socialists. There were only two kinds of people, builders and destroyers. Socialists were the destroyers. Builders knew themselves to be accountable to God.

I wanted to become a Christian and endure the consequences of my decision. All true believers have to suffer to be destined for heaven. I did not want to become comfortable in this socialist purgatory and then go to the actual burning hell when I died.

I needed supernatural intervention and transformation. Self-discipline has its merits but also its limits, and I had very little of it anyway. I had heard and observed some who had made significant advancements in life through their training and good works. Still, when they hit the ceiling of their personal energy, they started to ruin what they previously had achieved.

According to our tradition, you had to convert in public or in a church meeting. I was shy and could never do that. Did this mean I couldn't become a Christian?

In despair and overwhelmed with guilt, I went to my trusted secret place, the crab-apple tree garden. Kneeling under a tree, I prayed. Then, I sat down and thought. Then, I prayed again.

I confessed all the sins I could remember, and I asked God to forgive me and whether He could give me the courage to become a Christian. To be saved, I needed the courage to perform that prayer in public, or so I thought.

I cried my eyes out for hours. The next day, I did the same – I hid in the garden, knelt down and prayed. So it continued for three days, but I still could not find the certainty that I could do it.

On the third day, whilst kneeling and shedding bitter tears, I suddenly felt a gust of wind brushing over my head. It was as if an enormous hand had swooped through the trees and then through me. All the noise stopped, and it became calm. I could not cry anymore, and I felt at ease and very light. There was no sadness or regrets left in me. On the contrary, a joyous emotion started to well up inside me.

Then I felt it. He was here. The Powerful Presence. This time He was not judging me. He was accepting! Loving! I turned around and sat down under the tree. Was it my imagination, or was it real? I do not know. I did not see anyone, but He sat down beside me and placed His hands on my shoulders.

I loved every minute of it and said, "Thank you, Lord! I am so grateful to You! And I love you with all of my heart!"

He replied, "I know. I AM, and I am with you. All will be good."

It dawned on me that I was not speaking audible words. I was conversing in my thoughts. This was great. I could talk with the Almighty in my thoughts, and no one could hear us! No people, no demons, no angels, no one! It was the most private and secure communication in the universe. No one but God could read my mind, my thoughts. I did not need to worry about others' eavesdropping.

God was not in a hurry and said: "I am not restricted by time or space." He just sat there and was mindful of me without neglecting anyone else in the world at the same time. How magnificent is that!

We sat there quietly, forever. Then, He said, "Do not be afraid." After that, I became a changed and more assertive person. I now knew that I had what it took to become a Christian. Since that memorable day, I have never felt alone in life. He is always invisible, there with me.

～

In the next youth group meeting, two of my friends, two cousins, and I knelt down and spoke a sinners prayer in public. Now we would be recognized by the church as true converts.

Upon returning home, I met Abdil and Papa at the front door of our house.

"How was the youth meeting?" they asked.

"Good," I said. "We had five people praying the sinner's prayer."

"That's so good!" said Abdil.

"What are their names?" asked Papa.

I listed everyone by name and included myself.

"Praise the Lord!" said Abdil. "You know, now you need to go and tell everyone the Gospel, as The Bible says. As a child of God, you need to go public in the marketplace, on the highways and throughout the world and preach the Gospel to all creatures."

"All creatures?" I thought, and I looked at our dog, Sharik. I was not sure he was a creature that would get it.

In the evening, I went to my friends and said that Abdil had quoted The Bible whilst urging us to preach in public. One of them, Richard, decided to come with me the next day to try this. Richard was actually the son of Simul, the man I had helped to steal the money from.

Early in the morning, we met at the end of town where the highway started. We lifted our hands in an attempt to stop passing by cars or trucks. We called ourselves "The Hitchhiker Evangelists."

A truck stopped. It was a jolly fellow from our town.

"Where are you going so early, boys?"

"Take us to Beresovka." (Literally: The Town of the Birch trees, 12km away.)

"Sure, hop in. So, what are you up to?"

"We are evangelists. We tell people that Jesus loves them and that he forgives all their sins. Jesus loves you too, and you can go to heaven when you die! But you need to ask Him for forgiveness and repent from your sins first!" Excited, we interrupted each other as we imparted our knowledge to the bewildered sinner.

He just burst out laughing.

"Guys, slow down. Aren't you the kids of the Baptists in our town? Don't some call you The Sectarians?"

He ground the gears, shifting them up, lit up a cigarette and said, "Okay, I got that. I am a sinner. Now, tell me more about how I, the sinner, can be saved?" For the rest of the trip – about 40 minutes – we talked, and he smiled, laughed and asked the occasional question. I noticed that the radio in his truck did not work. In retrospect, I am not sure if he was honestly interested in our preaching or just enjoyed the unexpected entertainment.

As he dropped us off in Beresovka, he wished us luck in our mission endeavours. Emboldened with such tremendous evangelistic accomplishment, we crossed the highway to the opposite side and waited for our next victim.

A beat-up truck stopped. Richard opened the passenger door and asked if the driver would give us a lift. He told us to hop in. We did. The man was dirty and fat. The cabin was filled with cigarette smoke and smelled terrible.

"Just you two lads, travelling by yourself?" he asked grumpily.

"Oh, we are evangelists, and we tell people about Jesus!" We replied eagerly.

He looked with scorn at us and said, "Whaaaaat? What in the devil's world are you yapping about? I should report you and your stupid parents to the government for religious propaganda. I do not want to hear a word from either of you about that!" he demanded.

We shut up and looked startled. He drove for several kilometres, and then stopped suddenly.

"Get out, you fools. I can't stand your company. Off you go, ignorant sheep." He left us standing on the highway.

We stood there, a little daunted. We were surrounded by nothing, just fields and forests. It was a hot day, and the sun was at midday. We started walking towards home. Then Richard said, "That was our first persecution!"

I agreed.

We walked whilst periodically looking back in the hope that someone would come our way. For about an hour, we did not see anything or anyone. It was hot, and we had started to discuss if it would be wiser to cut across the fields and through the forests, but we could get lost.

Whilst having our discussion, we heard the noise of a faraway transport. We looked at the horizon and saw something. The hot air from the highway had a mirage effect, so the image appeared to be elevating in the air above the road. We waited another 15 minutes until we realized that a bus was coming our way. The highway was full of potholes, so no one usually drove faster than 40-50 km/hr.

The bus stopped next to us and the bus driver opened the door.

"You want a lift, boys?"

"Yes, please!" we pleaded in unison.

As we jumped in, the driver asked us, "What are you doing here in the middle of nowhere?"

"We are travelling evangelists," I said aloud, but with some caution now. I had read this phrase in a book about missionaries in Africa.

The driver and the passengers exploded in laughter, but we felt they were not so hostile as the last object of our evangelism.

So the driver said, "Okay, okay, here we go... tell us what you have to say. The radio is broken, and the passengers are tired of my singing," and he laughed even more.

We stood close to the driver in the passage and delivered our message. It was something along the lines of stop sinning, pray to Jesus, go to church and read The Bible.

We were so hot and tired that we could not talk much or stand for long. An older lady watched us the whole time and smiled from ear to ear, exposing her mouth full of steel teeth.

"Come here to me, boys," she said. As we took the seats at her side, she produced a bottle of cold water and gave it to us. I remembered that Jesus had said somewhere that you would be rewarded by God as a prophet if you gave a glass of water to a prophet. Of course, we weren't prophets, but it sure tasted good.

CHAPTER 16
BAPTISM AT MOONLIGHT

- 1972 -

A year later, I was baptized. The town was very restless again. Many zealous communist volunteers roamed the streets at night, looking for bigger group gatherings. Those groups could be Christians, and they would report them to the KGB for a reward. It was agreed to gather outside the town at 11 pm for the baptism. It was a dark and cloudy night. Then we walked without lights to a dugout pond. The water was muddy and used for feeding cattle. During the day, church volunteers had ensured no cow pancake dung was swimming on the surface. We sang some hymns quietly, and someone said a short sermon on the importance of being baptized as a believer in Jesus Christ.

When I stepped into the water with 5 others, the moon looked out from behind the clouds and smiled. It was midnight.

The person baptizing me asked, "Do you believe that Jesus Christ is your Saviour?

"Yes," I said.

"Do you accept Jesus as the Lord of your life?"

"Yes."

"I baptize you in the Name of Father, Son and the Holy Spirit."

He pushed me down into the muddy waters. We dried up, changed, split into smaller groups and tiptoed back to town.

We gathered again back in the safety of our neighbours' house. All who were baptized kneeled down, and the ordained brothers prayed that we would receive the Holy Spirit. According to the doctrine and tradition of the underground church, the steps of salvation were as follows: first, you publicly pray the sinner's prayer in church. Second, you share your conversion with unbelievers. Not many did this. Third, you complete a course of fundamental doctrines and traditions of the church. Fourth, you are to be baptized in the waters and finally, the prayer of an ordained brother would result in you being supernaturally filled with the Spirit of God.

Only then could you ask to become a church member. At the church meeting, you would stand up, and any one of the members could ask you any question about anything. Whether it be life, faith, morals, attitude, etc., they would vote on you if satisfied with your answers. By a majority, you would be admitted into the church membership. Only then could you claim to be a genuine Christian!

I felt very emotional. It was a long day and night.

Walking home from this meeting in the twilight of the morning, I stopped at the crab-apple tree garden, looked up and said, "I love you, Lord!" Only God could have given me the strength to go through all the rituals and traditions, become accepted by the church, and become lawless in a socialist society. I was 16 years old. The law of the land said you cannot be baptized before 18 years old.

CHAPTER 17
DRIVING LIKE A RUSSIAN

- 1973 -

After 8 years of compulsory Soviet schooling, I finally had enough. At 15, I got shift work as an oven heater at the commercial bakery for the local cooperative. Papa was the lead mechanic, which made this possible and gave our family cheaper coal, bread and an extra income.

"You need to acquire some kind of a trade," Papa said. Our parents gave us a choice. My problem now, as a 16-year-old, was to decide what to do next. I was tormented by too many interests and ideas, but the socialist reality helped narrow my options to a pragmatic "Life-Calling."

My sister, Lyda, applied to become a nurse and passed the written entry exams with excellence. When she took the oral exam, one of the panel members said, "You did well in the exams. Your knowledge is impressive, but do you believe in your heart that the world originated as described in Darwinian evolution?"

"No. I believe in a loving God, who created a beautiful world and us humans." She answered honestly.

"Well, with that attitude, you cannot be a nurse. We need workers who base their views and work on science, not myths."

So she was denied study. Lyda's worldview was not politically correct. Her dreams of becoming a nurse were never realized. This was their game. To make it impossible for Christians to study, then call them uneducated and primitive bigots.

I saw how impossible it was for my older siblings Yasha and Lyda to study a decent profession, even though they had 10 years of schooling and outstanding average marks. Yasha travelled 800km away to the city of Tomsk University to study engineering. No one knew him that far away. But after two years, he had to break it up. Having only 8 years of schooling, I personally did not see a lack of opportunity for higher education as a disadvantage. A simple trade was an excellent choice, I thought.

After listening to a smuggled musical tape of traditional German folk music, I wanted to apply to a musical college. My friend Peter and I listened to it for days on end. However, musicians in the USSR played atheist Soviet songs, and the morally liberal student life was not suitable for a young Christian.

Then, my childhood dreams of becoming a professional pirate were revived after my peers went to a sailor's academy. I would have become a sailor just to wear that dazzling uniform. The majestic Irtysh River was only a day's trip from our town.

The beautiful hydrofoil boats, called Rocket, were used to transport passengers on the Irtish River. With a breathtaking speed of up to 70 km, they were faster than the busses on the highways. It was the pride of Soviet production and the first in the world. There was also an abundance of work on the barges, but a sailor's life had an awful reputation, too.

Our sovkhoz (soviet collective farm) got a delivery of several brand-new blue "Belarus" farm tractors. Anything that had wheels and moved fascinated me. I could see myself behind a steering wheel in a dusty field producing bread for the bright future of communism, but then Papa suggested that he could get me into a 6-month truck driver's school in Kachyry. I agreed it was a more suitable choice. So, at 17-years-old, I went to get my truck driving licence. It was about 70 kilometres from home and situated on the magnificent Irtish River. The program was a mix of in-class learning and mechanical garage training. A soviet truck driver needed to have the ability to repair his truck and source parts that were required. Then, he had to tell the dispatch if he was ready to work or not. Trucks were usually parked at home and were also used to do some extra jobs on the side.

We were a class of 21 teenagers. Unfortunately, the three girls who trained to become truckers were regarded by all other students as free pickings. Every morning, another fellow would recall the details of the previous night. I was repulsed by such an open display of immorality, and I hung around the workshop or volunteered to drive with the instructor a lot. It was one of those rare places where I did not make any friends.

My driving instructor was a short, round man who was always jolly and usually slightly flushed. He never stopped talking. The engine's roar, the rattle of the old truck and the noise of his voice melted into a particular hum.

All the wisdom and experience of his life was generously offered to me.

"Young man. To be a good-no... to be a professional trucker, you have to master two skills."

He stopped, looked along the road we were driving, and asked, "What do you see?"

"Well, I see the road, potholes, dirt, stray dogs, trees ... " I tried to be observant.

"No, no, no, no, stupid!" he screamed, "Do you see those nice red boots and the beautiful legs in those boots?" He was making extra big eyes at me.

"If you are a professional, you will always, always, always ..." he smirked, "Repeat after me, ALWAYS!!! See every beautiful pair of boots walking along the road! Do you get it, dummy?" He paused, shaking his head in disapproval. "And maybe, just maybe, you can also offer a ride to those enchanting boots. You know how public transport sucks in this town! You need to do a lot of good. Kapeesh?"

"Secondly, to be a trucker is a profitable job. A clever trucker will never experience want. You are a master of transportation and connections. There are a lot of things that need to be moved. A lot of it will be useful to you. You will live well! A trucker is the most courageous individual. He grabs his luck by the horns and makes all his desires come true!"

Papa had organized a place for me to stay with an old Russian Christian babushka. The small clay-house was half sinking into the ground, and the half above ground was lean. This was some nice extra income for her, and she took good care of me. Babushka Maria cooked delightful and simple meals. One time, she went to visit her relatives. I cooked for the first time in my life without Mama or Lyda looking over my shoulders, so I decided to make an omelet with baking soda. It grew huge in the pan and tasted quite awful. After spending an unusually long time after that meal in the outhouse, I decided that cooking was for women. A man's chief responsibility was to find a good wife that could cook.

Babushka Maria returned the following day. She had the urge to share the experience of her journey, so I listened patiently.

"My nephew drove his motorcycle drunk, like a maniac! So, he killed himself last year and almost died. If he continues driving like a dumbhead, he will certainly kill himself again, but this time, he will perish!" she exclaimed, crying.

Confused by this kind of logic of death and accidents, I asked Maria if we needed water. Four blocks down was the Irtish River. We carried all the water we required daily by hand. Grabbing the buckets, I went to the river. I took my time, sitting on the rocks and admiring the beauty of the sunset over the river. Then, after filling the buckets, I made my way slowly back.

Walking into the yard, I noticed the gate was open. Unusual, I thought. I walked into the house through the open door, and I found Babushka sitting on a chair in the kitchen, looking scared and frazzled.

"What's up?" I asked.

"Oh, it is so great that the good Lord sent you away. There was a horrible fight right in front of our house. One of the guys tried to escape by running into our yard and through the house ... he was almost killed, here on your bed. Those Satanists are always beating and killing each other all day long!" she cried.

I started to clean up the room and told Maria to calm down. It was undoubtedly disrespectful for me to talk to an old lady that way, but she was in hysterics and would not calm down. I heard a slap in the face would snap a person out of hysteria, but I would not dare do that.

Crime was rampant in this town. So I double-locked the doors and gates, and after a prayer for angel protection, we went to rest.

The next day was Sunday. As usual, the few believers gathered in Maria's living room. I was the only male, and because women were not allowed to teach in church, I did the bible readings and preached every Sunday for those 6 months. At home, our Sunday church services traditionally had three sermons. The custom was that you had to preach if you were a male and a church member. My friends and I began to preach as soon as we were baptized at 16. The first two sermons would be by teens or youth, and the last by a seasoned preacher. He would then correct or explain if one of us young evangelists got stuck or lost for words. So, we learned public speaking from a reasonably young age. But in this church, I was the only main speaker.

∽

AFTER GETTING my truck driver's license, I started to haul grain and water for our sovkhoz. Dima, a fellow trucker in his thirties, made the long-haul tours through our region. His truck was old, and the back axle would vibrate violently and give him headaches.

It was a bitterly cold February night when he stopped at a remote station. In the trucker's guest house, he got a room with another trucker. They did not know each other, but a close friendship developed after they warmed up at the wood stove and had sausage, black bread and a couple of shots. The stranger told him that he had just got a brand-new axle for his truck. It was something almost unheard of in our progressive socialist industrial reality. Both were very tired, so they hit the sack, and the stranger fell asleep immediately.

But Dima did not sleep. A glaring opportunity stared him in the face. He got up, packed his bag and went outside. Working through the night in minus 30 degrees Celsius temperatures, Dima managed to swap the back axles of both loaded trucks. Then he left before dawn.

Dima was so cold and frozen that he could barely drive. He turned into the next small village and knocked at the first house, where he saw the lights on. An attractive woman opened the door and let him in. She took good care of him and nursed him back to life. Dima spent a couple of days with her. He healed. They fell in love and married.

Dima was pleased that in one night, he had scored twice. A brand-new back axle for his truck and a brand-new woman for his life. This man had a clear understanding of life's priorities and the courage to force the hand of Lady Fortuna.

Hearing Dima's story, I thought, "I want to be as professional as Dima." Now I understood what my driving instructor meant when he said, "A trucker is the most courageous individual. He grabs his luck by the horns and makes all his desires come true!"

CHAPTER 18
BOGOMOL THE SOLDIER

- 1974 -

"You have a choice of two years of military service or three years of imprisonment," said the commissar, still studying my documents. I understood that if I continued to claim my religious beliefs as the reason for not being willing to bear arms, I would quickly end up in front of a judge. By all means, it made more sense to serve two years in the military. If they sent me to the army, it would be two years. If it was the navy or air force, they would require three years of my life. As I was a "sectarian," it would almost certainly be the regular army.

I was eighteen in the summer and drafted in October. Being drawn to serve the Mother Homeland was a regular part of life if you were a male and over 18. It was cold, cloudy and snow covered the village streets and houses. I felt sad, chilled in my soul and uneasy. Two years seemed like forever.

A farewell meeting was organized. Many from the church came

to say goodbye. It was an affectionate occasion. Friends prepared a small scrapbook filled with handwritten well-wishes and encouragement. They also gave me a mini, maybe an inch-square in size, Gospel of Mark printed in the underground secret printing presses. Mama prepared a lot of tasty food. We took pictures, sang songs, talked and prayed. I was leaving the safety of home for the first time. My head was shaved, and my bags packed.

I noticed my parents were a little embarrassed that I was so emotional. I am a crier. They both went through wars, exiles, prisons, and labour camps and lost their friends and family through the horrors of the "just and caring" socialist regime. Maybe they had hoped for a son who would display more bravery and courage by going into the "red dragon's den." Alas, this one was born close to the rivers of water. Perhaps that's why I had dreamed from childhood about sailing the vast oceans.

My angst over never returning home was fed by the occasional coffins received by dead soldiers' families. The caskets were made of tin and welded shut. Under the watchful eyes of military officials, who stayed until the coffins were securely buried in the ground, the coffins could not be opened. Our custom was to have open caskets at all funerals, but not in these cases. Parents and relatives had to trust in the explanation from the army as to the cause of death. The USSR was not at war, but military games were conducted in a real war-like fashion. Up to 10% of casualties were acceptable, I was told. Whatever the cause of death was, they all died a hero's death.

The other fact that concerned me was that Christians were murdered in the military. Being openly Christian invited discrimination, disadvantage and imprisonment. I had read a well-known story about a young soldier named Ivan in a handwritten book. He was a great witness to the gospel of Jesus Christ. He went through a lot of abuse, humiliation, torture, and in the end, he was drowned in a lake. In his last moments of life, an officer who was present said, "He was a courageous man and a real believer."

"You are going into the army as a boy, but you will come back as a man," a lot of adults told me. They were trying to cheer me up. If I come back at all, I thought pessimistically.

My cousin, who had finished his service not long ago and now ran a CNC machine shop, said that he did not want me as an apprentice.

"After the military, you will be a mature person, and you will know what responsibilities are. Then, I will be interested in training you and giving you a job," he said.

The other expectation placed on me was to get married as soon as I returned home. After military service, at 20-21, all men married as quickly as possible. Relatives, parents, and the whole community played at active matchmaking. Conventional wisdom said that you would become a drunkard if you didn't marry as soon as possible after returning from the army. For us Christians, alcohol was never an option. So we married very quickly, had many children and became active in the church.

It was prestigious to have a girlfriend waiting for you when leaving for military service. It was a classic romantic notion: a soldier is defending the motherland, and a young girl waits longingly for her hero to come home. I liked a pretty girl from our church. She was the daughter of Simul and was of a different nationality. So, I asked her if she would wait for me for two years.

"When I return, will you marry me?" I asked.

She looked away and then to the ground and said, "No! But if you wish, we can talk when you return." Maybe she remembered that years ago, I was involved in relieving her father of some cash.

I never did return to my hometown. For the rest of my life, I never asked another girl to marry me. Even my wife, Erna, I am married to today, I never asked, "Will you marry me?" Instead, I gave her a diamond ring and said, "We need to organize an engagement party, so everyone knows." She agreed.

Shaved and a little bewildered, thousands of us were crammed into a dilapidated building in our regional capital. We went through another round of interviews and medical and physical check-ups.

The most annoying part was having to stand naked in rows while waiting for your turn to be examined by the doctor, while a bunch of nutty nurses gawking, giggling and whispering.

Then came a one-on-one interview with a commander. I glanced at my open file in front of the young officer and saw in big red letters "sectarian". I knew that this was not a good start. The officer did not say much. He wrote in my file for a while and then said: You will serve two years.

Every day a train full of new recruits would leave. The large building got emptier by the day. Finally, I was loaded on the last train.

"Where are we going?" I asked an officer.

He barked, "None of your business, youngster!"

I tried to read the names of the train stations to guess what direction we were travelling. We were slowly moving west. I felt relieved. My oldest brother, Yasha, had served his time in the southern Asian Soviet Republics. He had experienced a rough time, so I did not want to end up there.

After a week, our train stopped in Lviv, Ukraine. We disembarked and loaded onto trucks. In three hours, we were standing in front of a military barracks in a forest. The air was soft and forest-juicy green. No snow yet, just rain. This is a different climate from the harshness of Siberia, I thought. Somehow I felt fortunate.

"This is a training school. First, you will go through a 'Young Soldier' course. Here, we will make you soft mama's boys into soldiers." The sergeant was yelling and trying to look scary. They planned to achieve these goals in three months.

First, we had to approach a table and empty our bags and pockets. Then, the trainers would sort our content, throwing some into a vast garbage bin because those things were "not permitted." Some goodies they'd take for themselves later. The rest we could keep.

Before I unpacked my bags, I asked for permission to go to the outhouse. It was located behind the Bania (Steam Sauna) building.

Between the bricks in the wall, I hid the mini Gospel of Mark and the notebook from my church friends.

Then, we sat on a stool, and a soldier shaved all our facial hair off with a mechanical shaving machine. Then, we stripped and went into the Bania. Washed clean of our civil past, we emerged on the other side and were given our uniforms. We looked ridiculous, like scarecrows in oversized and unfit rags.

The daily routine of training began. Get up, run 3 km, wash and dress, line up, breakfast, training in various technical areas and shooting our SKS's and AK47's on the range. This was PVO, anti-air defence troops. We had two different types of earth-to-air rockets: S-125 truck-mounted and S-200 stationery.

The spooky forest around the barracks was even darker after hearing the tales of horror. Two years ago, a group of Ukrainian nationalists had supposedly snuck into these barracks and cut the throats of all the soldiers inside. No one escaped.

The food was not enough. The Soviet Scientists designed food for soldiers that was apparently sufficient, but my stomach disagreed. From a rural lifestyle where we had everything fresh and aplenty, this tasted like rubbish. We were constantly hungry. Upon leaving the mess hall, we would grab any piece of black bread that was left-over. At night when there were lights out, we chewed our pilfer under the blankets.

I also used a small pocket light to read my notebook, the gospel of Mark, and pray.

One day upon returning to my bed, a sergeant stopped and commanded me to go to Politruk's office.

"I see a Baptist for the first time in my life!" he greeted me. "We never had a nut like you here before. This is a disgrace. A complete embarrassment for our battalion." The officer was an old fellow and looked annoyed. His face showed his love for a stiff drink. It was as if he was saying, "I really do not need this to finish my career."

He must be close to retirement, I thought. Then, he showed me the confiscated notebook and the gospel of Mark. My sergeant had discovered them by routinely inspecting the sleeping quarters.

"You will keep quiet about your religious delusions. You are not allowed to talk to anyone about this, understand? We will change your mind and make a decent human out of you and a defender of our values and our motherland." He barked one sentence after the other. As if I did not understand Russian, he repeated every sentence, but much slower and louder. "Now, get out of here! Sectarian!"

In the following weeks, I found I had a new routine. In the little free time, we had, when most soldiers spent time messing around, watching TV, and telling jokes, I had to sit in front of an angry, overeducated officer. He described how glorious the atheism of socialism was and how dumb and stupid faith in a God was.

The more he argued, the more my love for religion grew. Deep down, I was a little petrified of what this insane individual could do to me, but on the other hand, I started to pity him. He looked miserable and confused – a damned, lost soul. Jesus loved him too and could have been his Saviour if he wished. I tried to convey this to him. It was counterproductive. His anger turned into rage, and his volume increased to such a level that the soldiers outside could hear him scream. I didn't take it personally. He had to do the job for which he was receiving a decent salary. Sadly, and most likely, he really did believe in the atheist socialist propaganda that he was spitting out so energetically. I was not sure who the real sectarian was here.

[1]

---

1. Bogomol means in Russian a God Worshiper

CHAPTER 19

PRAYER AND PROMISCUITY

- 1974 -

The three months of training passed, and we were transferred into regular units of service. I was assigned as a personal chauffeur to Politruk (political commissar responsible for the political and ideological education), Pavel Alexandrovich. He clearly saw in me a challenge to his professional skills. He was determined to reprogram a delusional Bogomol (a God worshiper) into an atheist.

For the following year, my main job was driving the jeep for the top brass of the battalion, primarily for my dear Politruk.

He was a charismatic, attractive, 35-year-old stud. Every week we would drive 40 km to Lviv to pick up women. As I understood, they were all married to other officers. They were young, attractive, and playful. After picking them up, I was told to drive to a building, a park or into the forest. They would go out a short distance and enjoy themselves. I would look the other way and hope the singing of the birds would drown out all other sounds.

All military brass liked to have an exuberant amount of entertainment, ladies, gatherings and cocktails. I often had to carry my esteemed colonel home on my shoulders to the second floor of the officer's compound, where I would hand him over to his young and charming wife.

By that time, it would usually be past midnight. I would then drive back to the barracks as slow as I could. These were precious moments of freedom and time to count the stars and converse with God.

Being from a small town and a family with clear conservative values, all this was wildly worldly and offensive. I never thought that highly educated, well-off, privileged people were living such perverse and hypocritical lives. It was Sodom and Gomorrah. My parents had raised us to know the difference between a godly life and a worldly life. This is it, I thought. Biblical values are black and white. This is black.

For any minor offences during your service, you could end up on the "Gubba," which was 10 to 15 days in a cold, wet and isolated single cell. For major violations, They would release you from military duties and send you to a Siberian labour camp for many years.

A lot of minor delinquencies were overlooked. There were hundreds of young guys between 18 and 22 years old. Energy and testosterone were flowing freely. Fights to establish rank or influence were frequently indulged in. We were not allowed to leave the grounds and go into town to mix with civilians. For this, you needed permission. It was given once a month for half a day or so. In fact, we were trained to think that our two biggest enemies were the West and the civilians.

"Samovolka" (self-allowance to leave) was a choice. You just slipped through the hole in the fence and went to do your stuff at night. Some sold truck parts, tools or paint on the black market and bought vodka. Others found friends or girlfriends and visited them.

The officers were mainly in their thirties. Most of them married and lived close to the soldier's barracks but outside of the compound. Their wives worked in different departments on the military base. Some as medics, others in the kitchen, as switchboard operators or in the offices. In those days, we had rotary phones, and the switch stations were also located on the base.

The officer's wives knew how to dress to make any soldier's blood boil. They enjoyed a lot of attention, and they didn't just work for the money; there was love in the air. After work, soldiers told many tales and argued over which officer's wife was the hottest. I guess the socialist dogma about everything belonging to everyone extended to women, too. You just needed to be discreet about the open secret. You didn't tell, but you knew.

As a soldier, you were paid three rubles a month. It was enough for toothpaste and some cigarettes. An affair with an officer's wife was a way to get some extras. This was all per the gospel of Karl Marx's Socialism: from each according to his ability, to each according to his needs.

Walking one late night from the AutoPark to the barracks, a sergeant stopped me.

"Teach me to pray," the sergeant said. "My grandmother was a believer. She had icons and candles in the corner of her room and always prayed for me."

I was not sure if this was a set-up or if he was honestly searching for God. Was he sent to see if I was engaging in religious proselytism? I looked up. The stars above us on this rare, clear night sky were bright and abundant. It seemed as if the heavens were open. We stood on the ice of a frozen pond near the barracks.

I looked at him and thought, "He is probably one of those uncommon individuals who can still think outside the box. The social systems have not yet enslaved his mind."

"You know our modern, progressive secular life. There is no room for religion anymore, but somehow, I need it. Without God, all this doesn't make sense." He continued to look around.

I decided it was worth the risk. So I said quietly, "Well, you just talk to Him."

"Don't I need to learn some kind of a formula of holy words to be heard?"

"No, He likes simple honesty," I said. "In fact, the Most High prefers short prayers. He gets tired of long ones. He especially despises those who just like listening to their own voice and repeating someone else's phrases."

"That's how it is?!" he wondered.

"If you want, I can pray first, and you can listen in," I suggested.

"Sure, I would like to hear a prayer again. Do it, man," he encouraged me.

Per my tradition, I folded my hands, closed my eyes, bowed my head low and spoke to God. The sergeant mimicked my posture and listened.

"Now, you say something yourself. Whatever you want to say to Him."

There was a short, awkward silence. Then Bohdan said, "I am not sure what to say, God. If you are listening and if You can forgive my sins, I pray. If you can, teach me to pray. Keep my mother and all the saints safe. Hear me, please. Amen."

We went back to the barracks silently and went to sleep. Now I had a secret brother in the faith.

Many years later, in Germany, my brother-in-law told me, "Bohdan was asking about you."

"Who?" I wondered.

"He said he was in the Army with you."

"Oh, Bohdan! I remember him. How is he?"

"Well, as you know, our church has many projects in Ukraine. A man approached me in one of the towns and asked if I knew someone with your name. He said he became a believer in God on that cold starry night when you taught him to pray. He is now active in the church, together with his family, and walks with God!"

It humbled me to hear this and made me tear up. An insecure young soldier, afraid of intimidation and treachery, gathered the courage to say a short quiet prayer in front of a stranger. The Spirit of God used it to change a life and make him a blessing for many. I live for moments like that! It is worth doing what's right, even in the face of fear. A verse came to mind, "Cast your bread upon the waters, For you will find it after many days." Ecclesiastes 11:1. (New King James Bible) I hope the Father in Heaven smiled!

CHAPTER 20
NO WAR, NO LOVE

- 1975 -

On Wednesdays, we had political training. Politruk, a young and knowledgeable lieutenant, was an excellent teacher. We went through Marxism – Leninism, Communist Party programs, the history of various wars and revolutions and international relationships. A lot of it was dry as dust. Especially the ideological atheistic propaganda part.

Most of us Christians in the USSR were pacifists. Taking up arms in general and swearing allegiance to defend the USSR, in particular, was considered morally wrong. You could not support a godless, communist, one-party, undemocratic system. There were a lot of debates, doubts and conflicts of conscience about it. Those who confronted the issue head-on in public were considered the biggest heroes of the Christian communities.

One Wednesday, I was about to get a dose of sobering reality. We were at the end of World War II history lessons. I already knew that in the so-called Christian democratic-free countries, believers in God did not have the slightest hesitation at becoming policemen or soldiers going to war for their country's interests. These wars were branded by The West as "the just wars".

Twenty-six million Soviet people had died in WW2 – the biggest casualty count of any country involved. The USSR was weakened. Without Stalin's troops breaking the neck of the Nazis and pushing them back, the western allied forces would not have had the slightest chance of winning the war. Alas, that did not deter them from devising a devious plan named "ShipDrop." It was a plan to drop up to 466 uranium bombs to annihilate the entire Russian population! Similar bombs had been tested already. Those bombs were called FatMan and LittleBoy, and designers were delighted with the results from Hiroshima and Nagasaki, with a quarter of a million civilians dead.

Over 100 million people still lived in Russia at that time. Just two weeks after the war with Germany ended, US General Lauris Norstad submitted an "Atomic Bomb Production" memorandum to president Harry Truman. Luckily, the US did not have enough carriers or bombs available to execute the plan in time.

My father and mother were 22 years old at that time. Both were still in Stalin's concentration labour camps. Many suffered, and millions had already died in war and under socialist terror. The only solution that the Christian, democratic and freedom-loving societies could develop was to engage in genocide of the survivors? A mercy killing?! I did understand that they hated Stalin and his politburo and his successful occupation of half of Europe. The Allies were about to stage a Nuremberg process to punish the fascists who had committed genocide and "crimes against humanity." They were now prepared to do the same as what the Nazis did.

We were glad that spies had smuggled the formulas and designs of the atomic bomb to Stalin, and he had managed to build some. This established a balance of insanity by installing fear in Western arrogance. It also gave my siblings and I a chance to live. Thank God for double agents. The world was not divided between the axis of evil and the bastion of good. It was gray and sinful. Sin is universal and disregards national and political borders. Anyone who wants to sell his soul to the devil can do it anywhere.

The lecture was over, and we went outside to breathe fresh air. I felt disturbed and disgusted after what I had heard. Guys started smoking. I needed to move away, so I began wandering. Governments, Christian or atheistic of any stripe, are all the same, I thought. They are immoral, corrupt and bloodthirsty. They want me to give my life for their stupid ideas. I reached the pond where I had prayed with the sergeant and looked over the small, peaceful city. If you do not stop them, these ideologues, these lazy bureaucrats, will grow to engulf all of life and then destroy it. They do not have noble goals; they have an agenda: plunder and destruction!

After lunch, I left the mess and went to the back of our barbed-wired high fence. I knew where the gap in the fence was and, after making sure no one had seen me, slipped out. Yes, it was illegal, and a soldier was not allowed to leave the compound without authorization, but I didn't care. Walking for a few kilometres on the railway tracks would take me right to the Christian family house that had "adopted" me.

Aunt Masha greeted me loudly, "Surprise! Surprise! Our soldier is here."

I could drop in anytime and be warmly welcomed here. Ukrainian hospitality is legendary. Everyone assembled around the table in the yard. Delicious perogies, borsch, smetana, tea, and sausages appeared on the large table. Uncle Oleksiy also arrived home from work, and loud laughter and conversations filled the air. I was so happy to be with my adopted Christian family. I felt accepted and at home.

Masha and Oleksiy had four children. Olga, the oldest, was eighteen and shy but flirtatious. This added another positive dimension to my visits. Her parents did not hide their eagerness to acquire me as a potential son-in-law. After a good meal and a few prayers, we sang a song and settled down to talk. Oleksiy started to cross-examine me about my family and parents. He liked that we were a close-knit Christian family. I had five siblings. We were underground Baptists, the correct denomination for Oleksiy, and Papa was a presbyter who had spent time in prison. He suddenly asked what nationality I was. All our passports stated our citizenship as USSR and the race of the person.

"I am a German," I said. "Our ancestors were invited by Queen Katherina the Great about 200 years ago. They first settled here in Ukraine. They prospered and had a perfect life here. When the Socialist Bolsheviks came, they took everything away and exiled them to Siberia. Today, I actually can't even speak German."

All went quiet. A cold gust of wind blew through the trees and flowers, and it became chilly. The sun was setting. Masha did not say a word; she just got up and started to clean the table. The kids went to play ball. Olga gave me a sad look and went to help her mom.

"We heard the Germans have horns on their heads," Oleksiy tried to ease the tension and laughed. He continued, "You know, in the Great War, some fought with, and some against the Nazis and a lot of horrible things happened ..."

What a conversation killer. It was the wrong answer, I thought. Oh man, I have the wrong nationality. There will be no more nice food or laughter and no future romance. The visit was over, and after thanking the hosts, I left. I returned to this family only one more time to say goodbye after being discharged from my military service.

I walked through the dark. As I passed a train station lit by lamps, I noticed the Military Police looking for someone. Disappearing in the darkness of the park, I sneaked by unnoticed.

Arriving back in the barracks, a sergeant remarked, "Soldier, your boots are full of dirt. Did you go to the whore house again without my permission?"

Everyone found it funny. At this time of my service, I was a "candidate," and no one, except a "Ded," had authority over me. I grabbed a "greenie" and told him to clean my boots and sew a white-collar to my gimnasterka uniform.

The two years of military service were unofficially divided into four stages of six months. Each stage could make or break you.

First, you were a "greenie." In this stage, you were a doormat to everyone and anyone. You worked double shifts, cleaned everyone's boots, washed others' uniforms, cleaned toilets and washed other drivers' trucks. You "happily" did anything, no matter how humiliating it was. If you didn't like spitting your teeth out and running around with a bloody nose, you forgot how to talk back, period. At that stage, I once tried to argue with the sergeant. Three nights without sleep while peeling potatoes in the kitchen was too much, I said. Then I discovered that I could fly. That night, the fourth one, my eyes did shut, just not from lack of sleep.

The second stage was the "ladle." It meant you were less harassed, but you were still an underdog.

The third stage was that of the "candidate." No one really bothered you, and you could order others around, but you did not have the authority of a "Ded."

The fourth and last stage before going home was "Ded," literally meaning "grandfather." You were untouchable even by the officers. You commanded unlimited respect and authority. You could demand anything from anyone, and it would be done immediately for you. There was a particular Ded who enjoyed laying in bed and watching TV on Sundays. He would ask one greenie to bring him a glass of drinking water, splash it on the floor, and then ask another greenie to mop the floor. Then he would repeat the fun again and again.

The discipline and effectiveness of the army depended on this unofficial but powerful structure.

I crashed into my bed without attending the obligatory evening line-up and check-up. Falling asleep, I pondered the meaning of, "What is war and what is love."

CHAPTER 21
A DESERT ROSE

- 1975 -

The Warsaw Pact war games were commencing in the desert. After several days of a train ride, we disembarked. All our gear and equipment arrived, and we unloaded and organized our living quarters and our rocket launchpads. For the following several weeks, sand, wind, sun, and heat were our environment. Food became extra crunchy, and our tea was cloudy.

Spotting some East German soldiers amongst the ranks, I walked over to greet them. Considering myself of German descent, I tried to display my best German. They looked perplexed, unfriendly and did not understand me. Turns out my German was non-existent. I tried Russian, and they did not speak it either. What a bunch of dopes, I thought. They don't even speak the most beautiful and rich language in the world. All NATO troops speak English. Warsaw Pact soldiers are obliged to talk Russian! What's wrong with these clowns? Walking back to my troops, I thought again, What a twisted world!

All my life, I was called a Nazi pig. In Ukraine, my romance ends because I am of the wrong race. Here the Germans do not accept me as one of them. Who am I?

My assignment was to drive a major around in my jeep. I was to be with him 24/7 and even sleep on the floor in the town apartment where he was staying. The major was not from our battalion. He was friendly and had a relaxed attitude about things. I was pleasantly surprised how well the 4x4 wheeler GAS69, a Russian military jeep, was performing. We had few roads and needed to drive through a lot of sand dunes. I always liked driving, but the desert and dunes added an extra level of enjoyment.

One day we had a high-level brass visit. General X, from Moscow, was observing the exercises. As the aircraft began to approach us, flying low over the dunes and making loud noises with their guns, our men launched the counterattack. A beautiful display of multi-coloured explosions, burning planes, and fiery crashes opened up before our eyes. General X and a big crowd of officers happily commented and congratulated each other on a well-completed mission. Suddenly, something went wrong. On one of the rockets, the self-contained guidance system failed.

The rocket shot into the sky, then plummeted down and started to dance like a drunken Genie over the dunes. Sometimes it came alarmingly close to the command tent where we were stationed. Mortal fear gripped everyone – these anti-air rockets were designed to explode about 10 meters before the target. Every missile was loaded with over 3,000 steel balls of various sizes, transforming the flying object into a sieve. Nothing within range survived.

Everyone fell to the ground and began to dig into the sand. It produced a dust cloud as effectively as if a bunch of lizards were at work. I looked up, and General X was standing straight and observing everything with a smirk on his face. It was said that he was a Vietnam veteran and had nerves of steel. The rocket fell at a fair distance and exploded without causing any harm.

When everyone got up, shook the sand off and gathered, General X grinned at the other officers, who looked a tad embarrassed.

"A little frightening, isn't it?" he quipped. Then, he gave some specific advice and suggestions and went to his jeep. Observing him, I was unsure whether he was so unhappy with his life that he had a death wish or whether he was just plain mad. He looked high on danger.

Not an average human. Definitely a creep or something, I thought.

My major motioned to me to get ready. I ran to my jeep and started it. As he jumped in and said,

"Drive to town, to the Command Centre (we had nicknamed it the Brass Booze Bar). Oh, *!&#$!*. We will all get destroyed at this upcoming briefing"(meaning the officers). Still, he did not at all look troubled. "Then, we'll get wasted. General X is tough but has a sense of humour about things," he chuckled.

The major got out in front of the Command Centre. Before I could move, a girl appeared in front of my jeep and hit the bonnet with her open hand. My major looked at me and made a funny face. The next second she opened the door and sat beside me. At the same time, my driver's door opened, and a Military Police officer (MP) looked at me, then at the girl.

"Papers please, soldier," he said, not taking his eyes off the girl.

I saluted and pushed the gas pedal, leaving the MP standing in the dust with his mouth open. In the mirror I saw him lift his hands in frustration, then turn around and walk away. I noticed he did not write my number plate down, which meant I was safe.

Now I could take a better look at the girl. Oh, my ... oh, my God! She was stunning! A light dress, a desert rose in her long dark hair, dark eyes, and what a smile! Her face, her figure, everything was right. I forgot to breathe. She was about my age (19) – a native Asian beauty. No sweet perfume ever tortured me more, and then she turned to me.

"Darling, I know a cool place outside of town. I have a snack and something to drink. Let's have a good time!" She said it as if we had known each other for ages.

The sound of her voice was as if warm honey was running straight into my soul. Oh yes, she had that right; I was thirsty and hungry – in more ways than one. And here I was, offered a banquet of everything bundled together in an elegant package. She had total control over me. She was a delicacy, and she knew how powerful she was.

My traitor eyes gave away my appetite.

"Why?" I squeezed out, unable to speak intelligible words and sounding like a man on a wheel of torture.

"Oh, dear boy, don't be shy. You are so handsome! My soldier! Defending my freedom. I want to have a good time, and say thank you. Be grateful..... drive!" she commanded.

In these circumstances of dirt, heat, sand and war games, she was a stark contrast. A desert rose! She smelled good and looked like an Arabian desert princess out of a fairy tale. With her eyes and smile, she was killing me softly. My blood rushed into my head as I was battling with my conflicting emotions. No, this was not a wicked temptation. She was a holy angel entering my life! I was losing my mind.

"What's wrong, my love? Why are you slowing down?"

I stopped the jeep and tried to find an excuse, murmuring that I needed to go on duty and pick up an officer in the field.

"You are so stupid! Why are you doing this to me?" Her open hand turned into a fist. She got teary and realized that I was dumping her. I felt more sorry for myself than for her. I asked her to leave and drove off.

I drove to the apartment and, without taking a shower, laid down on the floor in my sweaty and sandy uniform. My stoic posturing was gone. My eyes were wet, and I felt sorry for myself. The girl's eyes, face, smile, laughter and figure lingered vividly before my eyes. I felt like a cruel and heartless monster. At this moment, I hated being a conservative Christian. "Why do you tempt me, God?"

I screamed. "I am a man, and red blood runs in my veins. You created me as a sexual being and then devised morals to cage me in?!" I was angry with God.

"You ask for sacrifice ... Yes, this is my sacrifice." I experienced the primary principle of sacrifice in real life and sacrificing what was lovely, pleasant and precious to me on that day to gain the better, more authentic and superior blessing of the Divine in the future. A lesson that always stayed with me.

"Dear Lord, don't do this to me again, please! Next time I will take that 'Sacrificial Lamb' for myself. Did You see her? Can any sane man resist such sweetness? No, no, no ... I am an utter fool to let a cherub-like her fly away!"

I lay quietly for a while. Then I continued, "Don't lead me into these kinds of temptations again!" I felt the futility of this request. I knew He would not honour it. "Okay, then do this for me, good Lord; every time I get into these situations, make me stupid. Send your angels to spoil the chemistry of the affair, so I do something turn-off-ish, to be considered ugly, to say silly things, to ruin the spark ..." I felt at peace. I guessed He agreed. To give honour to Him, He kept this promise and fulfilled it throughout my life. I am now very skilled at looking, acting and talking stupidly.

Exhausted, I fell asleep. That night I dreamed of rain in the desert, of a garden in the sands full of roses, of a gorgeous Asian princess, but love and time ran through my fingers and exploded in the empty blue skies.

The major shook me awake.

"We need to go. You look awful. It must have been a wild night. Didn't I tell you these Asian girls are great?"

We drove back into the desert to learn how to kill, burn and destroy.

CHAPTER 22
STAYING ALIVE

E duard shot himself with his SKS carabiner while on duty last night," the unit commander announced. "He had a letter in his hand from his girl saying she is marrying his best friend."

Eduard was a withdrawn and hard-working guy. He was always conscientiously trying to do everything right and was never involved in scandals. Last night, while he was on guard duty alone in the tower, melancholy took over and ended his life.

"That was stupid," said one soldier, "he should have gone home and blown out the brains of this whore and the traitor friend."

"What a waste!" said another.

"You should not pay with your life for the wickedness of others!"

"If you want to sacrifice your life, do it for something worthy, not for evil people ..."

The soldiers were in shock, and everyone tried to make sense of it as best as possible.

Eduard's remains were gathered and sealed in a tin casket. An officer and a soldier were ordered to deliver the coffin to the family. They would assure them that their son and brother had died heroically on duty while defending the interests of the USSR.

I was appointed to replace Eduard on shift the following night. So I went to our weapons depot and signed out my SKS carabiner. I had a long night to think, and I meditated on life and death.

Killing is so wicked. It is different when the days that God allotted for you have run out. Eduard must be very ashamed now, standing in front of the Almighty, who probably asks him, "Why did you shorten the life I have given you? You missed a lot of good that was in store for you in the future." What will he say – "Because I had a bad day?" How embarrassing that must be! Now he cannot correct it anymore. Murder is a sin; it doesn't matter whether you murder someone else or yourself.

Morning came, and I went to breakfast: tea, one sugar, black bread and a small ball of butter – tasty! As I was leaving the Mess Hall, I was tired and not paying attention and didn't notice my former boss walking into the building.

"Soldier!" screamed my beloved colonel, Pavel Alexandrovich. "You have become too relaxed! You have never learned to respect me.

Salute me properly! Now! Again! Again!" His frustration at being unable to convert me from a God-worshiper to a Lenin-worshiper had grown into a rage. This was probably the moment he needed to vent. I saluted a few times and stood at attention.

The hypocrisy in his life and the virtues he preached stressed both him and me out. I had lost respect for him, and he knew it. He needed to change his tactics.

"Idiot!" His shouting was so loud that the other soldiers and officers stopped to watch.

"I have enough proof to send you to the GULAGS for a good number of years! You wasted and sold military property and damaged the defence ability of our country."

Oh, I thought, that doesn't sound good.

We had just returned from war games in a desert. The tires on my jeep were worn away from driving for weeks on dunes and rocks. This was supposedly the evidence of me selling good military tires to the civilians in that region.

Alexandrovich looked angry and, at the same time, somehow sad. He paused and then said more quietly, "If they had not given me a promotion to a higher rank, I would have followed your case through and put you away for a very, very long time, but now I have no time to do so. I have to move to another region in our country. Lucky you. Now, you ugly vermin, disappear from my sight."

He turned on his heels and walked away. That was the last time I saw my beloved colonel, Pavel Alexandrovich. I thought Promotions are good! Especially when they happen to your enemies.

The following day I was summoned to the main office, and the new Politruk said that I would be his driver for a while. His name was Captain Valery. He was more of a philosopher, and he liked hearing himself talk. That was okay with me. He never barked out his orders. I also liked him for not having to drive him to wild parties as often as the others.

One day, when returning from Lviv to our base, we drove along the railway lines. A passenger train was gathering speed. I squeezed the Soviet GAS 69 for all it was capable of and overtook the train. Then, I let off and drove the speed limit. Valery was quietly observing me.

Then he said, "Hm, how little a man needs to be happy!"

We laughed.

"You know, soldier, I like you a lot. You are very different from others. Your work ethic, punctuality, cleanliness and honesty are commendable. You don't swear, don't smoke, don't get drunk – but one thing is missing. You need to become a Komsomoletz. I can arrange that. You can have a great military career if you join The Communist Party."

Komsomoletz was a communist youth organization.

"Captain, If I join the Komsomol, I will become like everybody else. I will assimilate and change, and you will not like me anymore," I replied. With Valery, I felt I could be more honest and straightforward.

He just looked at me.

"Hmmm, maybe you are right," he murmured and sank into his philosophical musings again.

∽

HARVEST TIME WAS APPROACHING AGAIN, and our battalion was going to do agricultural work. The collective farms in the USSR couldn't manage all the work themselves, so classes in school were cancelled, and kids were sent to help harvest veggies and other crops. Some of the military and their trucks were also sent to villages to help out.

An average soviet collective farm (a cooperative agricultural enterprise operated on state-owned land by peasants who lived in that village) was around 8,000 acres. An average population of about 3,000 could not manage it by themselves. They needed a lot of help. Compare it with, say, a Canadian family farm of 1-2,000 acres that a single-family can successfully manage.

The soldiers looked forward to it. It was a kind of holiday and away from the rigid military routine. Moreover, it was in a civilian setting with good food, parties and girls. Most of our battalion was dispatched to Ukrainian towns and villages.

Along with a few others who had misbehaved, I was left behind to take care of the base. It was intended as a punishment.

Outside of town, we had an underground command bunker and a launching pad for the rockets. The elite unit of officers ran that post. Every day a military truck which was modified into a bus took them to and from work. The chief officer came to the main office and asked for a new driver for that bus. He had just put the previous one into jail for drunk driving.

"Well, as you know, most of our drivers are on harvest work," was the response.

"I need one for tomorrow. The one I had was arrested," said the captain.

"Only two are left. One is an alcoholic, and the other one is a bogomol (God worshiper). We suggest you take the alcoholic."

"No, no. Could you give me the bogomol? I had an alcoholic already," said Victor.

This job turned out to be my best year in the military. I drove exclusively for Victor. He was of Nordic nomadic nations, a seasoned officer, and had a relaxed attitude towards military hysteria. At the end of the working day, Victor would have a drink with fellow elite officers, and they would become a happy-go-lucky bunch of guys. So I drove, and Victor talked.

He asked a lot of questions and opened up about his life over time.

"Why do they call you a bogomol? Who is God, and who is Jesus? What does the Bible say about ...? I have done a lot of wrong in my life. Do you think God forgives everything and everyone?"

Several months passed. Victor was pleased with my work, and I was happy not to be harassed by officers who were still hungry for a career. By now, I knew all about his life, family and relationships in detail, and he knew all I could tell him about the Christian faith and the Bible.

"Why are you still a regular soldier?" he asked one day. "Did no one promote you to a higher rank?!... Ah yes, I think I know why," he laughed, "but I can give you a higher rank or two weeks off for a holiday, you know. What would you prefer?"

In general, it was considered embarrassing to return home from the army as a regular soldier. Many guys going home would secretly prepare shoulder pads with higher ranks of a Sergeant or even Lieutenant. When they sat on the train on the way home, they sewed them on and proudly pretended to be successful in their military career at home.

Expecting me to desire a higher rank, he said, "I will advise the Stab office to prepare the documents for a higher rank."

"Thank you, Captain, but I would prefer time off to visit my family," I had surprised him. "A military career is not for me!"

"What, you do not want a higher rank?! There are only six months left, and you will go home for good! However, whatever you wish. I give you two weeks plus a week for travel," Victor smiled, delighted with his generosity.

CHAPTER 23
THE RACE CARD

- 1976 -

I was the last one of my year's draft to be released from military service. It took a two-day train ride from Lviv in Ukraine to Valga, Estonia, to arrive home.

At the end of my military service in Ukraine, my parents and three younger siblings moved from Northern Kazakhstan to Estonia. Papa's logic was to stay at our older sister Lyda's house, unregistered with the authorities and wait for my homecoming. Lydia was married to Sasha, and they were legal residents of the Estonian Republic. Papa knew that people of ethnic German background were refused residency in the Baltic republics of Estonia, Latvia and Lithuania. The locals treated the ethnic Germans very kindly, but the socialist government had endorsed racial intolerance.

Since the Helsinki Final Act Agreement of 1975, it had become possible for relatives, separated by the chaos of World War II, to seek each other out and even to reunite. As far as we knew, no one lined up to apply to move to the USSR from Western Europe, but there was enormous interest from ethnic Germans hoping to leave the socialist paradise.

The Baltic republics were more relaxed and made it easy for many Russian Germans to emigrate to Germany. The communist government did not fancy this bleeding out of good workers and made it as difficult as possible. So, to emigrate, say from Siberia or other Asiatic republics, was almost impossible. There were stories of families repeatedly applying for 15 or 20 years. Refusal after refusal did not deter them from insisting on their right to live with their relatives abroad. I do not know if my parents had hoped to emigrate one day, but I certainly did not.

The first thing I needed to do was get a civilian passport and register my place of residency. In the USSR, you could not live without the government knowing and approving where you resided. I went into the local passport issuing and registry office and received a new red soviet civilian passport. I opened the first page, and it said "registered" in Valga. I went out and showed it to Papa, saying that it was all good for now. Papa took my passport, turned to another page, and there it was, "DEREGISTERED"! So, I was not legally permitted to live in this town. I turned and went back inside.

"There has been a mistake," I said to the woman who had just issued my passport.

She looked at me, smiling, and said, "No, there is no mistake here, young man. You have to move on and find somewhere else to live."

"Well, this is not right!" I protested.

"No, no, it is right. You can leave now," she insisted.

"You will hear from me!" Anger at this injustice was rising in me. I was a soldier of the glorious USSR and could live wherever I desired! Or so I'd thought, but apparently, I was mistaken.

"Oh, for sure we will ..." she laughed. Governmental bureaucrats had enormous power and privilege in an equal democratic socialist system. So she did not care. She had heard a lot of empty, frustrated threats.

We had heard that the Minister of the Internal Affairs of Estonia had a day of open-door policy where he received people from the public and listened to their complaints. Anyone could come on a first-come, first-serve basis.

Christians lived as close-knit communities and would assist and help each other with anything. Mischa, our church brother, had a Lada. He was a close friend, and with him, I had secretly transported some paper to the underground printing presses at night. We got in his car and drove to the capital of Estonia, Talin. We waited and quickly got an audience with the Minister.

Before the impressive, ornamented office door opened, I turned to Papa and said,

"Papa, don't say a word! I alone will speak!"

Surprisingly, Papa did not say much. He had a very dominant personality as an ex-prisoner and as a pastor who was used to leading and taking charge, but, to my surprise, he listened to me.

We went in. The Minister, in military attire, was sitting behind a big desk with two men in civilian clothes on either side. The two KGB civilians did not say a word but just examined us and were constantly writing notes. I guess there was some psychological profiling going on.

"How can I help?" The Minister asked in a soft baritone. Just the tone of his voice made me feel comfortable.

"I am a soldier who has just returned from my obligatory two years military duty to the Motherland and wanted to register in the city of Valga. They gave me a passport but refused to give me residence!" I said, handing over all my documents.

"You are of German nationality," he said, looking at my passport, "and Germans are not allowed to reside in Estonia. It has been like this for several years now."

"Yes, Sir," I replied. "May I speak? You are telling me that in defending my Homeland, my German blood would be good enough to be spilled, but to choose a place where I desire to live, my German blood is not good enough – with all respect, Sir!" I felt a fit of anger and frustration boiling within me.

The Minister lifted his head from my papers and looked at me with genuine surprise. His "bulldogs" on each side also stopped writing and looked a little puzzled. There was a minute of silence. Then the Minister said in his winsome baritone voice,

"Give it a week. Then go back to the office of registration," he smiled, "Now, you can leave."

"Thank you, Sir," I said, and we both walked out. The whole appointment took less than five minutes.

Driving back, we wondered what it all meant.

A week later, I took all my family's passports and went to the office in the city. There she was, the arrogant bureaucrat.

"Here I am," I said, handing her the passports. "We want to have residency here in Valga."

"Oh, yes! Good to see you, comrade." Her friendliness was in stark contrast to the previous visit. "No problem. Just take a seat, and in a minute, we will have everything ready."

She stamped all our passports with registration and permission to live in this town. She handed me back the passports and wished us a good life in Estonia. I felt a sense of victory, but she looked so pitiful. Like a whipped poodle, she hurried back to her cluttered desk. Middle management must be the most brutal stage in a career. Like being between a rock and a hard place, you do what's right according to the rules, but then the rules change. You look stupid.

CHAPTER 24
CIVIL DISOBEDIENCE

- 1977 -

Good handwriting, the calligraphic art, was admired by all. Our songbooks, Bibles, biographies and most literature were mainly handwritten. Mama had a printed Bible in old gothic German, inherited from her mother. After Papa returned from the labour camp, the KGB officer did return this heirloom Bible back to Mama, as promised. Papa, as the church leader, had a Russian printed Bible. It was illegal and complicated to acquire religious literature. The socialist freedom of the press meant that only ideas that agreed with the government agenda could be printed.

Typewriters were almost impossible to come by. They had to be registered, and anything typed could be traced to a specific typewriter and the person who owned it.

The churches solved this problem via the illegal, underground press movement. At first, they used gelatine printing. Books were produced that way cheaply, but the letters were smudged, not sharp, and hard to read.

The next step was an actual printing press. Some converts to Christianity had the advantage of having studied engineering before they became Christians. As a professing Christian, you had little chance of receiving higher education.

Books and encyclopedias were censored, and information on printing methods and technology was impossible to come by, but museums were open! The proud demagogues displayed how they had started the Bolshevik revolution, along with the printed pamphlets used to subvert the Tzar's government and disseminate their socialist propaganda. So, train tickets were bought, and many Christians travelled to Moskva. Museums with displays on the October Revolution and associated heroic adventures were visited. Here, the methods and technology of printing pamphlets were displayed and described in detail. Visitors studied and memorized the facts. Then, they went to an apartment of fellow believers, where they would write down everything they had learned and compare notes. It was a kind of industrial espionage.

Those who had engineering degrees and technical know-how designed a printing press. They repurposed washing machine motors, bicycle gears and chains, and other easy-to-come-by household items to make a prototype and then produce a series of printing presses.

Sourcing printing paper was the next challenge. Anyone who bought a large quantity of paper was suspect. Over many weeks, countless families would buy a few leaves of white paper and bring them to a designated house in the village. Periodically, a car would come by and collect the stacks of paper from several villages to take to the next town. Then, the piles of paper were transported to the secret location of the printing presses.

Each step was secret. We did not know the identity of the drivers, the printers, the engineers who would do repairs or the chemists who cooked the printing ink. We also did not see how the unbound, printed pages arrived back in our town. From time to time, our youth leader would ask a few of us to come to his house at night, and we would bind and cut bibles and other literature to size. Bookbinding was another fun, self-taught skill.

Tithing 10% of your income was an honour. No one spoke about tithing openly, but everyone participated regularly. We never knew where the money went, but we knew that it would somehow support the underground press, families of prisoners and those leaders who lived in hiding from the government. I knew of a few young people who suddenly disappeared from our neighbouring town's church, only to hear that they spent many years in hiding, printing bibles and eventually ending up in prison. If someone decided to go into the underground ministry, the only way out was either via prison or a cemetery.

Once, while still living in Northern Kazakhstan, we went to a Christian wedding in a neighbouring village, Konstantinovka. I only remember that Peter, the bridegroom, was napping a lot during the day. It was a long day, and the hot weather and extended church services dragged on from morning till evening. The poor guy could not stay awake. We didn't criticize him, but we found it amusing. A year later, I heard that he and his wife had disappeared. Many years later, he was in prison, and his young wife had died. The chemical fumes and closed, unventilated basements were not suitable for longevity. They had sacrificed their lives to print bibles and religious literature for their brothers and sisters in Christ.

~

After my military service, I joined my friend driving at night, transporting supplies to the concealed samizdat (Russian: Self-publishing) houses. Militia monitored and patrolled the roads constantly. It was a cat and mouse game. Gambling with our freedom, we broke the law in the name of God. Speeding through forests and fields, we had the advantage of knowing every back road and pathway.

On one occasion, we had a tail following us and needed to shake them off. We were loaded with paper. Our trusted vehicle, the Moskvitch with its 1400cc engine, wouldn't break down...we hoped. We pushed the pedal to the metal and held on with white knuckles. The Russian engineering did not disappoint. Our "racecar" howled loudly, and we began to lose the "garbage" (a slang name for the militia). There was a shortcut coming up, and we needed to gain an advantage in the distance. Around the corner, we took a sharp right, almost colliding with a tree, switched off the lights and disappeared into the thick darkness of the forest. The militia sped by, losing us over several sharp curves. We stopped at a designated place and unloaded all we had into a parked Lada. It was dark, and I did not see the face of the other driver. He was small and looked like a kid. Barely catching a breath, we jumped back in and sped off. As we drove onto the main road, the militia immediately appeared behind us. We shouted excitedly, "We made it! We are still in front of them!" The flashing lights went on, and they forced us to a halt. We obeyed. Jumping out, they surrounded us, shouting and gesticulating.

"Get out! Open all doors, and the trunk!" was the order.

My friend asked with a tone of surprise, "Comrades, what is going on?"

After checking and glaring at us, they were puzzled. Nothing in the car was suspect or illegal, but they knew, and they felt that something was not right. The officers went aside and consulted each other, then came back and questioned us. They looked again. Nothing.

"Why did you drive so fast?" they asked.

"Just going home. We like driving fast," was the answer.

"Okay, carry on, but remember, we are watching you."

We drove off, thankful to God for His protection and intervention. It meant He needed us to do another run. We believed that life and freedom would end only when you had done all God wanted you to do.

The underground printing press was discovered not long after this, and all involved, including the house owners, were arrested. A lot of literature was still salvaged by quick-thinking neighbours. These boxes and suitcases of printing material ended up in the homes of believers in our city, Valga. I had also brought home a bag of books, but Papa said I should make sure it goes somewhere else. He was the church leader, and the KGB would suspect him first.

We needed to get the literature out of our town as quick as possible. KGB was actively searching and looking. All roads to and from Valga had been blocked, and every car and truck searched. There was no way we could transport the literature without risking losing it all.

At this stage of my career, I was promoted from a long-haul delivery driver to a personal chauffeur of the director of the clothing factory. Now I was driving around the CEO in a luxury black Volga limousine. Everybody knew the director of the factory. The biggest employer in town and a very influential figure.

This Friday, my director asked me to take him and his family to the Datcha (summer cabin) and pick him up Sunday evening. It meant I had the Volga for the weekend.

So with my friends, we loaded to the max the black Volga with illegal Christian literature, and I drove it on the main highway out of town. Approaching a KGB roadblock, I slowed down. As the militia saw the Volga of the director of the Valga Factory, they energetically gestured me through and smiled from ear to ear.

I smiled too, remembering Psalm 23:5 "You prepare a table before me in the presence of my enemies; You anoint my head with oil; My cup runs over." Well, the oil was in the engine that day, and my heart was running over with joy.

A lot of printed material was saved that day.

CHAPTER 25

KGB ANGELS

- 1977 -

Life in Estonia felt modern and sophisticated, and nothing like Siberia. You could buy and acquire many more things. I started to adjust to civilian life, and it was good. I got a promotion from a long-haul truck driver transporting fur coats from the local dressmaking factory to the seaports in Tallinn for export. Now I was cruising in a black luxury Volga chauffeuring the Chief Executive of the factory around.

The youth group at our church was a lot of fun. We started a band, and for the first time in this church, we had a drum set and electric guitars. We bought jeans (it was not authentic denim) and experimented with different styles of music. I still wonder why no one in our conservative church spoke out against the worldly jeans, drums, e-guitars and singers with microphones. We performed during Sunday worship services. Often the electronics failed, and we were fixing problems in front of the entire congregation. Everybody just stood there or sat and patiently waited until we got it right. They wanted us to succeed. They were accepting and good people. I loved this church and this town. I wanted to live here forever!

A family from Belorussia moved to town. Their nationality was acceptable, and they did not have to go through the same loops as us Germans. They had two beautiful daughters – and were all non-Christians. As the second assistant to the youth leader, I readily made myself available to teach the older tenants of faith. From then on, I knew that theology could be sexy. Life started to become more colourful and enjoyable. I saw a bright future, but life has a freakish habit. Right, when you think all is good, that people need you, that there is a lot of good happening – then expect a hit in the solar plexus where it hurts.

Walking across the field towards home, I saw a "bobbic" parked in front of our house. A bobbic was a Gas69, a jeep usually used by the government or military personnel. It was a jeep I'd driven as a chauffeur for my officers in the army.

My heart sank. What is this? Oh, God!

You can be positive, speak affirmations, have hopes, but when the KGB parks in front of your house, you know that God has decided to test you, and in this case, the whole family, again. How sincere are you? Do you trust God? How strong is your integrity? Can you control your fear? Can you love your enemies?

WHAT IS the difference between a KGB and a Mafia? The government employs one, and the other is self-employed. Both are very profitable enterprises. Their methods are very similar: the end justifies the means. Their goals are also identical: ensuring the loyalty of the constituency. Both tend to make offers that you cannot refuse.

The KGB made such an offer to Papa.

"Again, Ivanovich, again, you are on the radar of the powerful! You are active in the local church, and that is not good. For you, we mean. The reports and complaints went over our heads to Moscow. It is only a matter of time before you are back in prison. This time we doubt you will come back," they continued, "We know of your German nationality. Many have emigrated already. We strongly suggest you leave the country, too. It will be good for you and will make our life simpler. Let somebody send you the invitation forms from Germany. Come to our office, and we will do the rest."

These KGB agents were of Estonian nationality and had different reasoning. It was a more polite approach. In the end, the outcome would be the same, but you felt better during the process.

As a family, we sat down, and Mama and Papa told us the news. Now the likelihood of us leaving the USSR and going to West Germany was a reality. I am not sure of my siblings, but I felt devastated. As far as I know, no one wanted to leave this beautiful Estonia. Everything was so great and promising here. A spacious house, good jobs, a great church, romantic relationships and relative freedom. Why did we have to go to capitalist Germany?

"Well, if we do not like it in Germany, we could move to other countries. I've heard you can do it. There is freedom. They are not socialists!" Papa said.

CHAPTER 26
ROTTING IN THE WEST

- 1977 -

"Why do they smile constantly?" I asked my sister Adina, who was sitting beside me on the airplane. "Why do they pretend to be so friendly?" We were on a Lufthansa flight from Moskva to Frankfurt. The stewardesses made me feel uneasy. Too much smiling was a sign of a mental disorder. And yet, somehow, I liked it. On soviet airlines, the stewardesses ruled over you. Here on a capitalist airline, they apparently wanted to serve you.

When leaving the USSR, we were told, "Western capitalist countries have corrupt values."

"They exploit the weak for profit."

"The police are brutal. They beat and shoot peaceful protesters on the streets."

"Out of shortage, they eat very thin sliced bread." (Later, we realized they placed a thick sausage on top of it).

"People are just cogs in the big factories of the bourgeoisie."

In short, the western countries were fast decaying societies. The capitalist system was on the brink of collapse and would shortly transition into glorious socialism. These, and many more, were the words that were said to us as we left for Germany. What turned out prophetic was that Western countries are now actively flirting with socialism – within just a few decades. This is very sad and worrisome for anyone who knows the difference between theoretical and practical socialism.

My parents and three siblings were about to discover a whole new world – the rotten, western bourgeoisie. Our oldest sister Lyda, her husband Sasha, and their two kids were also on the flight. Our oldest brother, Yasha, and his family lived in the Central Asian republic. They would join us in West Germany a year later. They needed to go through the cumbersome official channels. The Estonian KGB 'Angels' didn't only help us. Later, in Germany, we heard that the KGB also pushed out others who had been too publicly active.

After the visit of the KGB to our house in Estonia, we had only three months to dissolve all we had and get rid of all of our possessions. Relatives and friends came to say goodby, and we gave away all we had to them. Only a few suitcases were packed, and we left for the capitol Moskva. At the airport, we were again thoroughly searched. Border guards wanted to take away the last few photographs, but Mama got angry and told them off. Not expecting such a strong reaction, they backed away. Now literally having nothing, we were seeking asylum in Germany, a country of our ancestors. We resembled our grandparents, stripped of their farms and livelihood and then exiled to Siberia by the bolsheviks. We were refugees fleeing religious persecution in the USSR, so-called a democratic, just and socialist wonderland.

The food on the German airplane was unusual but tasty. The aircraft was clean. The other passengers were friendly. It was too superficial and sterile – no drunks, no fights and no profanities. What weird people!

We landed. The stairs were wheeled to the plane. The door opened, letting cool, moist German air in. It was September 1977, I was 21 years old, and we were entering a foreign land. The 'rotten' West! The smells, the people, the colours, and the way everything moved felt strange and enchanting.

I was at the front of the crowd of travellers walking towards the large airport building. Carrying our luggage, we approached the arrivals terminal, but we all were headed straight for a high glass wall! I frantically searched for a door. Not seeing a doorway, I slowed down and stopped. The stubborn Germans just passed me by left and right and ran straight into the transparent crystal glass. Suddenly, the wall opened and formed a gap.

"Ohhh my, Christmas trees and sticks!" I gasped. My head was spinning. My jaw dropped onto the pavement with a loud clack. I probably looked about as intelligent as a sheep, shocked when it returned home and discovered a new gate.

So many lights and such an array of colours! I was used to dark alleys and streets, and this was dazzling. Apparently, the Germans did not know there was toothpaste in shops. Oversize posters showed beautiful people with white teeth saying, "There is toothpaste – go and line up, or else you will go without." It was so excessive and redundant, but oh so charming and captivating. Typical wasteful capitalists.

Red Cross volunteers met us and invited us to sit down and wait for a bus. There were rows and rows of empty seats in a vast hall. Where are all the crowds? I wondered. The train stations and airports in the USSR were all crowded. The chairs looked like expensive leather. A man in a uniform asked my sisters if they wanted Coca-Cola. What?! I had always wanted to see a Coca-Cola.

When I was the chauffeur to the Politruk in the army, one of them told me about his trip to East Germany. The Soviet Army occupied East Germany, as the US and UK still occupy West (now unified) Germany. In East Berlin, he drank a Coca-Cola, and it was delicious.

I had always imagined a dark bottle with a brown bear on it as an emblem. As the Red Cross volunteer brought Coca-Cola and gave it to my sisters, it did not match my imagination. No bear on the sticker! It had red letters and no dark label. What a disappointment! The advertisers didn't even realize what could really sell Coca-Cola! I don't drink Coca-Cola to this day. If they change the label to include a bear, maybe I'll try it out.

An air-conditioned bus transported us to a camp for refugees. Upon arriving, we were given a free furnished apartment. The fridge was full of food. We were taken to a store with clothes, bedding and a lot of other beautiful things. All of it was free for us to pick and choose. There was a large eatery where three free meals were served. The capitalists really did their utmost to impress us, and we loved it. We had never been treated with such respect as humans. I started to suspect that I could actually love living in capitalism. Gratefulness filled our hearts for the German culture permeated with Christian (and not socialist) values. When we woke up from the sound of church bells on the first Sunday, I saw tears of joy in the eyes of my parents. Here, people were called to the church, not hindered.

We were confused by the tea bags. One of us insisted that you had to suck it; the others cut it and poured the content into a cup. A German cleaning lady solved the confusion by demonstrating the proper use. Apropos proper: Germans love this word, and it would haunt us for the rest of the time we stayed there. Right this and appropriate that, you had to do things proper and correct. Every little detail was so immensely important.

We admired houses, window decorations, flowers, lawns, fences, and cars walking through the small town. They were all so perfectly arranged, like in a museum. Clean, tidy and empty. Where were the people? I would stop and stare at a VW Beetle for hours. What was it? Strange and oddly attractive. Would I ever be able to afford a luxury like that? Later, I learned it was an idea from Adolf Hitler's imagination, and so was the autobahn. I did learn to appreciate speeding on the autobahns, but I never acquired a Beetle.

The prophetic words of Papa did come true, though. He said, "Well, if we do not like it in Germany, we could move to other countries. I've heard you can do it. There is freedom. They are not socialists!"

He was very correct. After some years in Germany, we all (except Lyda, our dear sister, who died in a car accident) used these freedoms. We travelled to multiple countries and lived, and still live, all around the globe. Australia, Canada, the USA, Paraguay, Brazil, and Malawi are just a few countries where we made our homes. Our children travel even more.

As Germans by ancestry, we had told ourselves that we were returning to our "homeland," but the Germans saw us as Russians. Now, in Germany, I was called a Russian pig. Wait, wasn't I called a German pig in Russia? I give up! I don't feel like I have a homeland. I do not feel loyal to any flag, country, political party, system or government. I am a world citizen, a vagabond, a pilgrim ... a citizen of another Kingdom! I trust no one, but I try to do good to those who cross my path in life. I believe there is a lot of evil, but I do try to practice loving all God's creatures, humans included!

Still, it feels so good to fester in the rotten West!

EPILOGUE

The sunlight on my face alerts my body clock and signals that it is time to wake up. Evergreens and fields of the prairies are covered with snow. I remember Mama saying that white snow covers the earth's dirt as the grace of God covers the world's sins. I think, *I am so glad that I am not living in a socialist sinister wonderland!*

A stunning princess walks into the bedroom and taps my feet with an open hand. She is beautiful! Long dark hair, dark eyes – and a smile! She is a delight, and she knows it.

Her voice is sweet like honey, "Darling, it is nippy cold outside. Our wood fireplace is ablaze. I have prepared a snack and something to drink. Let's have a good time!" She says it as a matter of fact – by now, we have known each other for decades.

I rubbed my eyes and think, I got what I like, and I like what I got, but she has no rose in her hair! In this freezing desert of snow, I can't find even one.

As usual, I pray before getting out of bed.

ANDREJ VOTH

Good Lord,
Where You are, there is a true paradise,
a wonderland of joy and fulfilment.
When governments respect your Word,
the people prosper.
There is a Law above any governmental laws.
When diabolical socialists take over control,
they imprison us in hell.
Let the intention of godless oligarchs be confused,
crushed and come to naught.
Deliver us from the evils of Marxism.
Let those who still have the "fear of God"
in them govern our nations.
Promote into power those who are unafraid to speak the truth.
You, God, are the only way,
the only truth and the only life we desire.
Amen

ACKNOWLEDGMENTS

I want to acknowledge everyone who helped me produce this book.

I would like to thank my wonderful wife Erna, who has remained a source of reassurance and patience.

I am also very grateful to my sons and daughter-in-law, who encouraged me to stop talking about books and start writing.

John Voth, you are a great editor. You helped me to say what I wanted to say. You know your dad.

Michael Voth, thanks for an appropriate and beautiful cover design. You are a genius.

Colleen Voth, thank you so much for doing the final proofreading and finding the details, which I couldn't.

John Wiens, thank you for your input, my old friend. As we both grew up in that monstrous empire, you understand me before I speak. That is more than I can say.

Peter Danzey, my dear Australian friend, I appreciate your thoughts and suggestions and admire your love of the Holy Scriptures.

Sally Kilby, thank you for editing and constructing cultural bridges between East and West. You have that tremendous skill to create order out of my chaotic scribbles.

Most of all, I am thankful to God, Who is the source of all life, all meaning, and all joy. You are the just Judge of the good and the bad. I adore YOU!

About the Author

Andrej Voth was born in Prokopievsk, Siberia and grew up under socialism. After attending eight years of the Soviet school system, he served in the army. Shortly after being discharged from military service, his family was forced to leave the USSR and settle in Germany.

Finding new freedoms, he explored and visited 30 plus countries and lived in four. He desired knowledge and graduated from academic institutions in Germany, Canada, France and Australia. Questions in world religions, anthropology, human rights, theology, and faith became his life passions. To support his global adventures, he worked various positions from caretaker to construction, from semi-truck driver to seminary professor.

Now, semiretired, Andrej and his wife Erna call northern Alberta their home.

www.andrejvoth.com

 facebook.com/andrejthegiant
 twitter.com/andrejvoth
 instagram.com/voth.andrej

www.ingramcontent.com/pod-product-compliance
Lightning Source LLC
Chambersburg PA
CBHW070044120526
44589CB00035B/2303